JOURNALISTS AND ENVIRONMENT NEWS

JOURNALISTS AND ENVIRONMENT NEWS

A Study of Newspapers

Dr. Raimole Abraham

KANISHKA PUBLISHERS, DISTRIBUTORS
NEW DELHI-110 002

KANISHKA PUBLISHERS, DISTRIBUTORS
4697/5-21 A, Ansari Road, Daryaganj
New Delhi-110 002
Phones : 2327 0497, 2328 8285
Fax : 011-2328 8285
E-mail: kanishka_publishing@yahoo.co.in

Journalists and Environment News

First Published 2010

ISBN 978-81-8457-226-1

PRINTED IN INDIA

Published by Madan Sachdeva for Kanishka Publishers, Distributors, 4697/5-21A, Ansari Road, Daryaganj, New Delhi-110 002, Typeset by Sunshine Graphics, Delhi, and Printed at Rajdhani Printers, Delhi.

Foreword

Environment has wider ramifications across the globe, if one part of the globe is affected by environmental destruction. Therefore, every citizen on this globe has the responsibility to protect the earth so as to protect him or her in the process. For this purpose, creating public awareness is one of the responsibilities of the mass media. Hence, in this respect, journalists along with media owners have to play a major role in educating the public, the government, policy makers and non-governmental organizations. In relation to their role as mass educators, journalists have to perceive environmental issues before disseminating them to the public. Therefore, the study taken by Dr. Raimole Abraham makes an attempt to capture the perceptions of print journalists with regard to coverage of environmental issues in Kerala, India. Hitherto, no systematic study has been taken up to study the perceptions of journalists on environmental issues in India, more so in Kerala. Kerala, a state known for the highest literacy coupled with high newspaper consumption needs to be studied in the context of journalists' perceptions of their role in news coverage. Further, the case studies given in the study make an interesting reading. The study is a significant contribution to the mass communication studies.

February 19, 2010

Dr. D.V.R. Murthy

Associate Professor

Department of Journalism

Andhra University

Visakhapatnam-530 003

Acknowledgements

I am extremely grateful to *Dr. D.V.R. Murthy,* Research Director, Associate Professor and Chairman, Board of Studies, Department of Journalism and Mass Communication, Andhra University, Visakhapatnam for his valuable guidance and support throughout the work.

I thank *Dr. P. Bobby Vardhan,* Head of the Department, Department of Journalism and Mass Communication, Andhra University, Visakhapatnam, for the encouragement and suggestions during the work.

I also thank *Dr. C. Ramakrishna,* Assistant Professor, Department of Journalism and Mass Communication, Andhra University, Visakhapatnam, and *Ms. G. Anita* and *Dr. C.M. Vinay Kumar,* Teacher Associates, Department of Journalism and Mass Communication, Andhra University for their support.

I specially thank my husband and children for the support and patience shown throughout the research work. I am grateful to librarians of various academic institutions who have helped me in my data collection and compilation work. Last but not the least, I thank all the print journalists in Kerala who figured in the sample of the study for their kind co-operation.

Dr. Raimole Abraham

Contents

Foreword *v*
Acknowledgements *vi*

1. Environment and Society 1
2. Environment and Media: A Review of Some Studies 20
3. Research Methodology 37
4. Profile of the Print Journalist 52
5. Environment, Print Journalists and Professional Obligations 64
6. Newspaper Coverage of Environmental Issues in Kerala 83
   I. Perceptions of Print Journalists
   II. Content Analysis of Select Newspapers
7. Case Studies 119
8. Summary and Conclusions 142

APPENDICES

I. Environmental Movements in India 165
II. Environmental Issues in Kerala 171
III. Questionnaire 177

Bibliography 190
Index 204

1
Environment and Society

Towards the end of the twentieth century, environment[1] has become a key area of concern at national, regional and international level. The exploitation of the natural world has been going on for centuries and at certain points in time, particular issues have come to be defined as mainstays of public concern (Anderson, 1997: 1). Because environmental destruction has been going on at a rapid pace, the life on the earth is increasingly being affected. The industrial revolution transformed the way of life as people flocked to cities to work in factories. The earlier dependence of people on agriculture slowly shifted to industry, which increasingly affected the environment. Forests were cleared to provide wood for new buildings and paper products. Larger amounts of minerals were extracted from the earth for industrial purposes and water use increased accordingly. Pollution, the by-product of industry, became one of the biggest problems, resulting in the destruction of nature (Graham and Chandler, 2000: 2).

Thus environment is part of a complex ecosystem, i.e., fragile and threatened by severe disruption from the competing forces of overpopulation, resource exploitation, over-consumption and industrial pollution (Melkote and Steeves, 2001: 192).

Brown (2003: 1) calls the earth a "planet under stress" with a "civilization in trouble." He wrote:

> We are cutting trees faster than they can regenerate, overgrazing rangelands and converting them into deserts, overpumping aquifers, and draining rivers dry...we are taking fish from the ocean faster than they can reproduce...plant and animal species far faster than new species can evolve, (thereby) launching the first mass extinction since the one that eradicated the dinosaurs 65 million years ago.

Moreover, religious texts often describe environment as an important part of human life and advises human beings to keep the nature undisturbed. For instance, the Hindu tradition lays emphasis on worshipping nature. Banwari, the former editor of *Jansatta,* a popular Hindi daily observed:

> The Hindu tradition describes three basic categories of forest. One is *shrivan,* the forest that provides you prosperity. Then there is *tapovan,* where you can contemplate as the sages did and seek after the truth. The third is the *mahavan,* the great natural forest where all species of life find shelter. Each of these categories must be preserved (cited in Prime, 1992: 10).

In India, people always had a harmonious relationship with the nature around. For example, it was *adharma* in ancient India to fell trees (Banwari, 1991). In traditional India, every village had a cluster of five great trees, known as *pancavati,* which represented the forest and they were said to symbolize the five primary elements—earth, water, fire, air and ether (Prime, 1992: 13). Furthermore, the preservation of the sacred grooves in India was symbolic of the pious feelings of the communities for the environment. For instance, *Chipko* (hugging a tree) *Movement* in India, which started off in the 1970s as a women's action for conservation of forests in the lower Himalayan region, became a major environmental movement spreading the message of environmentalism. (Appendix I)

With the enormous destruction of the nature, the humanity at large is increasingly facing the following problems (Chattopadhyay and Franke, 2006: 7):

- global warming;
- impending water shortages;
- declining area and declining yields of productive land;
- pollution of land, fresh water, sea water and air; and
- biodiversity loss.

Nevertheless, scholars like Thomas Robert Malthus, British parson and scholar in 1798 through the first of his two essays *On the Principle of Population* forecast an imminent environmental catastrophe arising directly from the pressure of population (Harvey and Hallet, 1977: 63). Moreover, Ehrlich and Ehrlich (1970) too considered population growth as a major contributing factor to the eco-catastrophe. Population growth exerts strong adverse pressure on the natural environment in the form of diminished forest resources, degraded agricultural soils, overgrazed rangelands, water pollution, diminished wildlife stocks, declining biodiversity and urban pollution. Because of population growth, the traditional practices of food would pave way to new patterns of agriculture such as mono-cropping, forests stripped for firewood and overconsumption of water. As a result, long-term management for posterity cannot be seen, and food demand is high (Stoez *et al.*, 1999).

However, another argument was that the technologies used in the past were ecologically faulty and were used without being aware of their ecological effects (Commoner, 1963). Further in 1970, Jay Forrester and Dennis Meadows examined levels of five chosen basic quantities—population, pollution, natural resources, agricultural capital and industrial capital—to indicate the state of the world system. The various positions that were adopted later on in the environmental degradation debate included categories like individual moral failure, the anti-science position, the pace of scientific and technological change, the spread of technological values, defective political-economic systems and the cost of economic growth (Harvey and Hallett, 1977: 82).

International Conferences

In this context, concerns were expressed at the international level on the quality of life being affected owing to increased environmental problems. In 1972, the United Nations Conference of World Leaders on Human Environment organized the first Earth Summit at Stockholm, Sweden to pave the way for further discussions and debates on environment related issues (www.unep.org). The developed nations, led by the USA, sought for greater efforts to protect the environment while many less developed nations feared that an effort to create strict anti-pollution laws in their countries would hurt their chances for economic growth (Steiz, 1990: 118). The developing nations of the world maintained that poverty was the main cause of deterioration of their environment in their countries (Steiz, 1990). Ten years later, the nations of the world met again to discuss about the global environment in Nairobi, Kenya. The positions of the rich and the poor nations had changed dramatically. The developing nations showed enthusiasm for further efforts to protect environment because they had seen that environmental deterioration such as desertification, soil erosion, deforestation and the silting of rivers and reservoirs was harming their efforts to develop and to reduce poverty. On the other hand, many of the rich nations led by the USA called for a slowing down of environmental initiatives until they had recovered from their economic recessions (Steiz, 1990). Further, a major inter-governmental conference on environmental education organized by the United Nations Educational Scientific and Cultural Organization (UNESCO) in collaboration with the United Nations Environment Programme (UNEP) in October 1977 in Soviet Georgia argued that problems of the environment were 'jeopardizing the development of mankind' (Rajalakshmi and Birundha, 1994: 265).

Subsequently, the United Nations set up the World Commission on Environment and Development led by Gro Harlem Brundtland in 1983. With the submission of the Brundtland report in 1987, environment became part of a new concept called sustainable development. The concept envisaged that while development is essential to satisfy human needs and improve quality of life, it should occur in such a way that the capacity of the natural environment to meet present and future needs is not compromised (Brundtland, 1989).

The United Nations General Assembly convened the United Nations Conference on Environment and Development known as the second Earth Summit in Rio de Janeiro from June 3, 1992 (www.unep.org). The primary goal of the summit was to find an equitable balance between the economic and environmental needs of present and future generations and to lay the foundation for global partnership between developed and developing countries, as well as between governments and sectors of civil society, based on common understanding of shared needs and interests (Cox, 2006: 68). A draft treaty known as the United Nations Framework Convention on Climate Change (UNFCCC) was accepted and signed by more than 150 nations represented at the Rio Conference. The treaty was finalized for ratification at this summit. The parties to the Framework Convention met annually in order to develop realistic mechanisms to meet the goals of the Convention. In December 1997, the countries that met in Rio in 1992 re-convened in Kyoto, Japan and reached an agreement known as the Kyoto Protocol, which called for the reduction of greenhouse gas[2] emissions by several industrialized nations below 1990 levels by 2008-12 (Agarwal *et al.*, 2000).

Further after ten years, another meeting was held under the auspices of the Conference of Parties to the United Nations Framework Convention on Climate Change (UNFCCC) and also by the Parties to the Kyoto Protocol in Bali (Indonesia) in December 2007. The Bali meeting proposed to achieve progress on a number of important issues relating to the Adaptation Fund, avoidance of deforestation through Reducing Emissions from Deforestation and Degradation (REDD), technology transfer, and Clean Development Mechanism (CDM) (Clemencon, 2008). Other events held at the venue discussed business opportunities in global carbon markets and provided a forum for countries to share experiences with national policies that have been put in place to meet Kyoto Protocol targets (Clemencon, 2008).

Environment and Development

Many nations in Asia, Africa and Latin America which became independent after the Second World War moved towards adopting the style of industrialized development. Large and small-scale industries that were set up as part of development agenda adversely affected the environment (Murthy, 2000: 13). The development projects recommended by the experts had their own consequences, both intended and unintended. For example, huge hydroelectric dams like the Volta in Ghana and the Aswan in Egypt that were developed in 1950s were able to produce needed energy for industries and provided power to the houses as intended consequences. However, these dams increased the spread of snail fever and water-borne diseases (Cambridge, 2002: 145). New varieties of seeds associated with the green revolution of the late 1960s in India increased the yield of foodgrains, reduced hunger and eliminated famine in the country. However, the new seed varieties required extensive use of chemical fertilizers, which polluted the water resources (Murthy, 2006:13). Thus environment and development are the two sides of the same coin (Sawant, 1993: 78).

Since the process of development cannot be stopped, damage to the environment can only be abated. Earlier, environmental consequences of a development process were considered separate from the social, cultural and economic issues. Slowly protection of environment was accepted as an important aspect of economic, political and social development (Sawant, 1993).

In spite of the plans suggested by researchers, academicians, development agencies and international bodies in different settings, development is incomprehensible and all the models of development are not holistic to offer a sustainable solution (Table 1). Even the most well meaning programmes will fail to yield results unless other dimensions like social and cultural are not given importance in development planning along with economic aspects (Stoesz *et al.*, 1999). Industrialization and urbanization have their own adverse consequences in development. These two issues, which were given importance in the modernization period, posed problems in the many parts of the world. For example, in India, the Ministry of Urban Development is focusing on new plans to decongest the cities in the country and is planning to encourage cycling in the urban areas (*Indian Express*, June 30, 2005). In this context, two case studies are presented here to showcase the failure of dominant paradigm while urging for alternatives.

Table–1
Development Models

Factor	*Economic Development*	*Social Development*	*Sustainable Development*
Goal	Growth with equity	Basic human needs	Growth with equity for posterity
Method	Free trade Exports Human capital Technology	Infrastructure	Input reduction
Organization	Multilateral banks, Development agencies, Private sector	NGOs, Development agencies	Polycentric (banks, Government, community organizations, international treaty organizations)
Science	Economics	Sociology	Ecology
Orientation	Technocratic	Humanitarian	Naturalistic
Focus	Extractive	Redistributive	Reproductive

Source: Stoesz *et al.*, (1999). *International Development*, London: Allyn and Bacon, p. 156.

Steel Mill at Nowa Huta

The setting up of a steel mill in 1950s at Nowa Huta in the Krakow region of Poland as part of the modernization model of development presents the failure of dominant paradigm in 1990s. Nowa means 'new' and Huta means 'mill' in Polish language and therefore the place where the mill was set up was known as Nowa Huta. The mill set up in 1950s and named after Lenin Steel Mills employed 40,000 workers. Since the Polish Communist Party set up the mill, it provided every aspect of the workers' lives. The workers were the highest-paid labour in the country; they were housed in subsidized apartment blocks ("Sendzimir Steel Mill, 1997"). Schools, hospitals, canteens and cultural centres were provided; separate units prepared hot meals for the workers and families below cost, another unit ran canteens, theatres, recreation centres as well as hostels and vacation hostels. There was a printing plant, a mineral water bottling plant and even pig-fattening farms. The town had all comforts except a church, and instead, they erected a statue of Lenin (Stoesz *et al.*, 1999).

The factory set up with the Soviet assistance began operation in 1952. The mill had all the integrated operations like availability of raw material at one end and the finished product at the other end. However, rapid changes in the manufacture of steel were taking place in the West, and spreading across the world, and steel mills at Nowa Huta, known as Sendzimir, was outmoded when it began operation (Perdue, 1995). The advances in the West did not reach the steel mills and the steel produced in the factory could not withstand in the face of competition from the international market. Added to this problem, the outmoded plant had another consequence: pollution. The levels of pollution in the area increasingly affected air, water and biological life. In 1980s, sulphur dioxide deposits were to the tune of approximately 1,700 tons per square kilometre. The Vistula river nearby at Krakow was virtually devoid of biological life (Kabala, 1985). In one school, 61 per cent children were under medical treatment for ear and respiratory ailments and Krakow had the highest infant mortality rate in Poland. Over 90 per cent of the workers suffered from some occupational illness (Stoez *et al.*, 1999).

In the late 1980s, with the political changes and consequent effect of easing of government controls, the Christian

Community of Working People was founded. At the same time, a group of academicians, workers, physicians, and journalists came together to form country's independent environmental pressure group, the Polish Ecological Club, which appealed for modernization of the Nowa Huta works to overcome the problem of pollution (Fura, 1985). With the outmoded technology and pressure from the environmental groups, the workers who were facing a dilemma of development, could not reconcile with the changes and yet they were not prepared to lose job security, cheap flats and food and freedom from responsibility of managing the factory. Despite the workers' anticipation for total modernization, a partial modification was carried out. Nevertheless, the workers hoped that the plant could be sold out for a huge sum of US $ 400 million; instead Sweden offered only US $ 7 million (Remnick, 1991). The government commissioned a study by a Canadian consultancy to explore a proper plan for the mill, and the study recommended the closure of the plant. Further, another study was commissioned in 1997 which suggested total privatization of the plant (Stoesz, 1999: 181). *The Financial Times* of London on February 1, 2001 reported 'Nowa Huta up for grabs'.

> Poland's mammoth Huta Katowice is near bankruptcy. Built in 1976 near the birthplace of then-communist leader Edward Gierek, the country's largest steel company produces low value-added long products and employs 7,000 workers in an industry where smaller, better-automated mills are becoming the norm. After a decade of failed deals and missed opportunities, Poland is buckling down to business on finding buyers for its steel industry, led by Huta Katowice. Warsaw is seeking foreign investors for stakes in four steel groups representing three-fifths of the country's steel output. Bids are due tomorrow and the government hopes a deal could be completed by as soon as the end of this year.

Campaigning for Bicycles

Modernization theories indicate that urbanization is one of the quickest ways to development of a nation, and Lerner's thesis (1958) for urbanization was believed to be a right indicator of development. However, urbanization proved to be a bane in the modern context. Urbanization has been increasingly affecting transportation and the following case study stands as a testimony to the ill-effects of urbanization. Urban environments require sustainable forms of transportation to overcome automobile dominance and congestion (Murthy, 2006: 37). London is an interesting case not only because its transport system is overloaded but also vehicle use is very high at present. London has 7.1 million people in 2001, and the city's transport authority, Transport for London, estimates that 27.3 million journeys are made in Greater London every day, with 8.5 million on public transport. Some 11 million journeys are made by car or motorcycle, 7 million on foot and 0.3 million on cycles (Castells, 1983: 319). London experiences the most intense and road congestion in the UK and air quality monitoring shows frequent breaches of national pollution guidelines for nitrogen dioxide and other compounds. Thus, the national picture has given environmentalists much cause of concern in recent years. The London administration and local boroughs control the entire transportation (Batterbury, 2003).

Nevertheless, the borough of Ealing has shown an example in controlling environmental problems. The borough contains a mix of residential areas, industrial estates and urban parks, several commercial centres and Southall, a suburb dominated by people of south Asian descent. Majority of the population use public transport and two per cent of the population use bicycles (Batterbury, 2003). Ealing developed a coherent policy towards environmental issues and employed a full-time sustainable coordinator to bring together community and local authority elements. Even citizens and non-profit groups involved in environmental issues of the borough. Traffic congestion, gridlock, strikes by transport employees and host of other issues drove citizens for alternatives. The promotion of urban cycle is a case in point. Since bicycle use was out of fashion on account of modernization, new technology, and high speed driving, 1960s and 1970s saw cycle out of daily use (Collins and Pharoah, 1974). However, people's awareness rose in 1990s on cycle use in London. At least, 300,000 Londoners keep cycling daily and five-mile ride on cycle is accepted to workplace (Batterbury, 2003). It delivers exercise to the body to keep good health, and it is sustainable and inexpensive. A non-profit organization, Ealing Cycling Campaign operating from a small central office campaigned for cyclists' rights in the capital city and thereby for improvements to health and safety through cleaner air, better bike facilities, and lower accident rate in London (see www.ealingcycling.org.uk and www.lce.org.uk). The campaign is gaining momentum to prepare for sustainable development. Litman (1999) commented: Sustainable development requires significant changes in our transportation system to increase economic efficiency, equity, and environmental security. Simply changing vehicle designs or improving traffic flow cannot achieve sustainable development. It requires changing the way transportation professionals approach problems and how individuals behave as citizens and consumers. Further, many such cycle campaigns have started in the UK such as Camden Cycle Campaign, to propagate cycle campaign to overcome urban problems.

Globalization, Environmental Movements and Mass Media

Globalization is increasingly occupying intellectual, academic and political discussions across the globe (Held, 2005). Although many scholars have given different interpretations to globalization, Hensman (2004) has aptly defined globalization as free movement of products, money, ideas and people around the globe. With the free movement of products and ideas, globalization in its wake has impacted the world in the economic and cultural spheres and this impact has been assessed in two different perspectives. One perspective is that globalization has positive results for the developed world and the transnational corporations, as they are able to expand their business ventures. Scholars cite mass tourism, migration, MacDonaldised consumerism and the spread of popular cultural forms in music, film and television as an example of globalization's influence on culture (Casey *et al.*, 2002: 112). The other perspective is that globalization has negatively impacted the developing countries in terms of displacement of people, loss of employment and marginalization of domestic industries and so on. For instance, the traditional artisan communities[3] (*visvakarmas*) in the federal state of Kerala in India are losing their identity as well as their sources of income because the federal government is withdrawing its support to the community as a fall-out of globalization depriving millions of craftsmen of their livelihood (Varghese, 2003).

However, globalization, which has opened new frontiers of knowledge with rapid dissemination of information on account of new communication technology, coupled with the growth of civil society, is held to be responsible for the emergence of new social movements in the fields of environment, human rights, women's rights and so on. Social movements, thus, represent a broad mobilization of interests around a particular goal (Anderson, 1997: 77). Further, any social movement, according to Ross (1998), originates depending on four factors: (1) a spontaneous collective response to rising expectations, (2) efforts to mobilize resources, (3) the effects of changes in social structure and political processes and (4) charismatic leadership. Because of these reasons, new social movements in relation to environment have emerged in different parts of the globe as a movement for conservation of the earth (Graham and Chandler, 1996), a movement for water conservation in the federal state of Gujarat, India (Shiva, 2002: 126), a movement for promotion of green consumerism (Anderson, 1997) and so on. For instance, in the state of Kerala in India, the 'Save Silent Valley Campaign' during the late 1970s and early 1980s, culminated in the abandoning of a hydroelectric project that included building of a dam, approved and on the brink of construction (Chattopadhyay and Franke, 2006: 185). The massive public campaign led by Kerala Sastra Sahitya Parishad (KSSP),[4] the strength of their arguments and the participation of hundreds of thousands of Kerala's people combined with the consensus of scientific opinion was reflected in various studies. In 1983, Silent Valley was declared a national park under the provisions of the Wild Life Protection Act of 1972 (Appendix I).

Table–2
Old and New Social Movements

	Old Social Movements	*New Social Movements*
Location	Polity	Civil society
Ideology and aims	Political integration Economic rights	Autonomy civil society News values/lifestyles
Organization of movement	Formal and hierarchical	Informal network and grassroots
Medium of change	Participation in political institutions	Direct action and cultural politics

Source: Martell, L. (1994) *Ecology and Society: An Introduction.* Cambridge: Polity, p. 112.

Though social movements are organized in a collective form of action, new social movements are contrasted with the old social movements in their organization (Table 2). New social movements have less rigid organizational structures, grassroots activism and pursuit of wider cultural and lifestyle changes (Anderson, 1997: 77). Therefore dissemination of information related to the movement will play a key role in creating awareness among the participants and outsiders to garner support to it, and the role of mass media is significant in this regard. For example, the movement of Asian textile workers in Los Angeles for better working conditions was successful because of an ad campaign (Delgado, 1996 cited in Ross, 1998). Because the mass media and society are interdependent, they reflect each other in their respective discourses. DeFleur and Ball-Rokeach (1989: 303) have observed that the mass media system is assumed to be an important part of the social fabric of modern society, and hence it is seen to have relationships with individuals, groups, organizations and other social systems. These relationships may be conflict-ridden or cooperative depending upon the mass media's perception of an issue which will influence the public opinion as seen in the Gulf crisis (Iyengar and Simon, 1997). Moreover, the mass media are assumed to be socially responsible to work for the welfare of the society, and therefore, the media are expected to support new social movements such as environment by setting an agenda for the government and policy-makers for action. Shaw and McCombs (1989) who suggested the agenda-setting role for newspapers observed:

> The agenda-setting role of the press is one of civic mobilization. The press helps focus our attention on the key problems of the day. It sets an agenda for action.

In the context of environment, newspapers can mobilize action by disseminating information related to certain environmental issues like solid waste disposal, air and water pollution, impact of population growth on environment, destruction of sea wealth, deforestation, destruction of public parks and so on which will have larger impact on the people, bureaucracy and policy-makers for solving the problems. Since a collective action from different segments of the population is emphasized to find solutions to environment-related problems, Harvey and Hallett (1977: 82) proposed some solutions. They are:

- changes in the attitudes and behaviour of individuals;
- a cultural revolution;
- the assessment and control of science;
- specific reforms in society's decision-making processes; and
- radical political-economic changes.

With these solutions in view, the role of mass media is increasingly becoming crucial in educating the public in the era of globalization, and in this context mass media's influence on new social movements in relation to environment is evident in some instances. For example, Rothman and Lichter (1990) found that negative media stories on nuclear energy policy had declined the public and governmental support to the issue in the United States. Furthermore, the mass media as a public educator are expected to play an objective and contributory role to highlight the issues to form an accurate opinion by the public, and press campaigns will help in formulating a policy by governments. Since public education is one of the key responsibilities of the media (Stuyck, 1990: 75), the media can frame issues while setting an agenda. Moreover, studies have found out that news media play a vital role in conveying information to the public about the environment (Byrd, 1997). While conveying information, the media can interpret and analyze the issues that have concern for the public. For example, a national survey in the USA examining the professional role conceptions of print and online newspaper journalists revealed the print journalists perceived the interpretive/investigative role as significantly more important than the online journalists. Thus journalists can interpret and investigate the issues that have a direct bearing on the humanity, while highlighting environmental issues. As early as 1963, journalism scholar, Bernard Cohen (1963) explained that the news media filter or select issues for readers or viewers attention and set the public agenda telling people *not what to think, but what to think about.* For instance, the *Daily Mail* in the UK took up the "Save our Seals" campaign in August 1988 and sustained it for over one year alerting the public and politicians about the need for environment (Anderson, 1997: 142). Prompted by a speech delivered by the then British Prime Minister, Margaret Thatcher on environment, the newspaper campaigned for saving the seals. Although *Daily Mail* campaign ended in 1988, the other newspapers continued the campaign. The content analysis of national newspaper coverage indicated that highest number of news items in the quality press was carried by the *Guardian* followed by the *Daily Mail* (Table 3). Once the *Daily Mail* launched a campaign, and demonstrated the strength of public interest in environmental issues, other newspapers followed. Anderson (1997: 147) commented:

It set an agenda for other newspapers. The seal virus, then, was used by the popular press as a peg to focus upon the environmental issues in the broader sense. The seal's story marked an issue-threshold for environmental issues, which were already attracting considerable concern from the public.

Table–3
National Daily Press Coverage of the Seal Virus During 1988

Newspaper	*Number of Items*
Guardian	28
Daily Mail	24
Independent	21
Daily Telegraph	15
Times	12
Daily Express	12
Today	12
Daily Mirror	10
Daily Star	8
Financial Times	5
Sun	4

Source: Anderson (1997) *Media, Culture and the Environment*, New Jersey, Rutgers University Press, p. 145.

In addition to setting the agenda, the media can continuously campaign the issues to educate the masses. In this connection the media have made important contribution to environmental issues. For instance, *Eenadu*, the largest circulated daily in Andhra Pradesh, India launched a water conservation programme named as *Neeru Meeru* in support of the state government's programme. The reason for taking up this campaign was that the newspaper set an agenda for itself. The coverage was positive for the programme. *Eenadu* in all its 23 editions allocated full page with the title, *Sujalam-suphalam*, to create awareness about water harvesting among people. Slogans, off-beat photos, messages from intellectuals and details from experts were published on the page. The paper announced a policy that every year it would start the awareness programme in April and would continue it till June 10 by publishing a full page on water conservation (Murthy, 2006: 84-85).

In Bangladesh, the media campaign helped the restoration of riverbeds which was occupied by influential people through landfills that narrowed the width of rivers (Anam, 2002: 270). Eventually the flow of water became constricted resulting in Dhaka's main river, the Buriganga, almost drying up. The river was also threatened by huge inflows of untreated waste. Newspapers launched a campaign to save the Buriganga and exposed how corrupt practices had allowed riverbank property to be sold to various private companies for commercial construction. In one case, the newspapers found that a major government body had encroached about 90 feet into river to build storage facilities for itself. The intervention of courts following the newspaper reports halted the work temporarily. Continuous coverage of pollution of the rivers led to greater public awareness about how negligence could lead to an environmental disaster (Anam, 2002).

The case of arsenic contamination of water in Bangladesh also was an example of the broad impact that the media can have. The *Daily Star* was the first newspaper to provide extensive coverage that included maps of the affected areas to highlight the gravity of situation. Researchers found that in large areas of Bangladesh, the ground water was contaminated by arsenic. The story broke in West Bengal, India, in the 1980s. Reports started to filter into Bangladesh that patients from bordering areas were going to Calcutta for treatment (Anam, 2002: 271). In the early 1990s, a group of doctors from Dhaka Community Hospital ascertained that arsenic contamination was indeed widespread and they approached the media to take up the issue. Estimates indicated that 60 to 75 million people in Bangladesh run the risk of being affected by this contamination (Anam, 2002). The print media were the first to draw attention to this issue and to make it into a major cause. Because of the media coverage, both the national government and the international community, including the multilateral agencies began to pay attention to the issue. The United Nations Children's Fund, the World Health Organization and the World Bank responded to the media stories and sent fact-finding missions to Bangladesh (Anam, 2002).

Environmental Journalism in India

In India, environmental journalism, which began in 1920s, received wide attention in the 1980s when academics, NGOs and social scientists took up the cause (Guha, 2002). In 1920, the Tatas were building a dam on one of the rivers in the Western Ghats near Lonavala, which was displacing some 15 to 20 villages. Senapati Bapat, a socialist from Pune led a satyagraha which was reported by *The Times of India* and the *Bombay Chronicle*. These articles took into account the wider argument mediating on issues like electricity for Bombay versus land for peasants, rights of displacement and large technology versus small technology (Guha, 2002). Further, M. Krishnan, who had a deep knowledge of India's biodiversity, wrote a fortnightly column for *The Statesman* from 1952 to 1996. He could write in a precise and evocative style by giving wonderful descriptions of nature all around. The period 1975-1985 was a vibrant period for the environmental journalism in India (Mazoomdar, 2006). For example, the industrial accident in Bhopal in India in 1984, which killed 3,800 people and injured more than 200,000 galvanized the news media to pay more attention to toxic chemicals (Detjen, 2001). In 1990s, the coverage of environmental issues grew in some parts of the country. Much of consistent environmental reporting in India has happened outside the popular dailies, weeklies and news channels. However, a big section of the regional language media, particularly in the South India, follows environmental issues rigorously (Mazoomdar, 2006: 159).

REFERENCES

1. Environment is defined as the natural environment which includes air, water, plants, animals, and thus natural environment is described in a word as "nature" (Graham and Chandler, 2000: 2). Tiwari (1998: 3) observed that environment is an expression of very wide amplitude that takes into account all those factors which directly or indirectly have a bearing upon the natural surroundings of human beings.

2. The build up of "greenhouse gases" (GHGs) in the Earth's atmosphere-carbon dioxide, methane, nitrous oxide and chlorofluorocarbons (CFCs)–due to human activities traps the sun's rays and heats up the earth like a greenhouse. Of these GHGs, carbon dioxide is responsible for over half the enhancement of the greenhouse effect. Carbon dioxide emissions, caused by the burning of fossil fuels are directly linked to individual lifestyles. The greater an individual's dependence on fossil fuels, the higher the per capita emissions. If GHG emissions continue to rise at present levels, global mean temperature is expected to rise by 1.4 to 5.8 degree Celsius by 2100 compared to pre-industrial levels, the sea level will rise by 9.88cm by 2100. Millions living in small island states and low lying deltas in Bangladesh, China and Egypt will be rendered homeless; there will be severe incidents of drought and floods, loss of biological diversity, reduced crop yields and spread of diseases to regions where they are not currently known to exist. Developing countries with less ability to adapt are twice more vulnerable to these adverse effects than industrialized countries, while small island states are three times more vulnerable (Agarwal *et al.*, 2000).

3. The traditional artisan communities include blacksmiths and goldsmiths in Kerala.

4. Kerala Sastra Sahitya Parishad (KSSP) is a committed group of school and college teachers, scientists and progressive minded citizens which fought the Silent Valley Project in Kerala.

2

Environment and Media: A Review of Some Studies

The mass media can play an effective role in educating the public in respect of environmental issues by covering them adequately and also highlighting them through newspaper columns. Yet, the mass media all over the globe, have not given much importance to the coverage of environmental issues although environment is the concern of everyone on the globe as pointed at various international conferences. For example, Ohkura (1995) examined Japanese newspaper coverage of environmental issues, focusing on the case of the controversy over the Isahaya Bay land reclamation project which was planned in the early 1950s while construction began in 1989. Although local activist groups began raising questions about the project in the 1970s, the newspaper coverage showed that the media played mostly a "spectator" role in the controversy, merely reacting to events. Further, in other parts of the world, studies found that there was lack of coverage of environmental issues in the media (Askari, 1995; Graham and Dziuban, 1996). Because the tendency in the media was to concentrate coverage on discrete, dramatic crises rather than ongoing phenomena (Schoenfeld *et al.*, 1979; Bendix and Liebler, 1991; Bowman, 1996) and sometimes misstatement or oversimplification (Sleeper, 1979; Carmody, 1995). Some reasons are obvious. First, much environmental news coverage is event-centered (Anderson, 1997: 121). Several researchers found that the news media are preoccupied with dramatic events such as oil spills and, to a lesser extent, pseudo-events such as publicity stunts

(Anderson, 1991, Wilkins and Patterson, 1987; Sachsman, 1976; Molotch and Lester, 1974, Rubin and Sachs, 1973). Second, environmental coverage tends to be characterized by a strong visual component because television news makes greater use of visual component (Wilkin's and Patterson, 1987). Third, news production tends to be closely tied into a 24-hour daily cycle while environmental issues tend to involve as lengthy processes. Television news broadcasts are based around particularly tight daily schedules and time acts as a major constraint (Schlesinger, 1987).

Further, many environmental reporters said that they and their media were committing less time and effort to environmental reporting (Detjen *et al.,* 2000). In addition, environmental beat is expected to be particularly difficult owing to rapid changes in environment. In the USA, a study in 1993 found that only half of the newspapers and 26 per cent of local television stations assigned someone specifically to cover environmental issues. Although environmental issues were covered, environmental reporters expressed reservation about quality of coverage. A study done by American Opinion Research in 1993 found that only four in ten print editors and even few reporters rated as good, the quality of reporting provided by other print organizations. Only three per cent rated coverage as very good. Among broadcast journalists, only 29 per cent of the news directors and 26 per cent of the reporters rated coverage from other broadcast outlets as good. Reasons for this included lack of good training programmes and difficulty in finding unbiased news sources (Detjen *et al.,* 2000).

In another study, Sachsman (2002) found that many newspapers did not have full-time reporters to cover environmental stories. Of the 27 newspapers with circulation more than 30,000, only 23 had a reporter covering environment on a regular basis. But the problem was that less than a third of these reporters had the word 'environment' in their titles. Most of them were general assignment reporters who covered environmental issues when they arouse. Specifically, this study found that environmental reporters were struggling to balance their interest in environment and their training to be objective journalists. While more than 98 per cent of these reporters agreed that they need to be objective as other journalists, 40.8 per cent said that reporters sometimes should be advocates for the environment and 30.5 per cent said that they should work with community leaders to solve environmental problems. However, many reporters had little background in most subjects, particularly in technical ones. Many of them wanted additional training in environmental law and regulations, natural sciences, environment economics and health risk assessment (Detjen *et al.*, 2000).

In Canada, Saari *et al.*, (1998) in their survey found that 105 of Canada's daily English-language newspapers and their commitment to science journalism revealed a general weakening and dilution of reporter allocation. Over 50 per cent of Canadian dailies did not allocate a science reporter. Only 18 full-time science reporters were identified. In a follow-up study of 45 journalists covering science news, at least half revealed the most covered science policy. The vast majority of journalists had no science training while time constraints and competing demands hindered professional development. Valenti (cited in Rogers, 2002) surveyed all the environmental journalists in New England and the Mountain West states since 2001. Specifically, 52 per cent newspapers in the Mountain West and 51 per cent New England newspapers had at least one full-time environment writer. About one in 10 local television stations in each region employed a full-time environmental correspondent. The other finding was that most environmental reporters were regularly taken off their beats to cover other topics. In New England, 18 per cent of environment writers said that they spend 67 per cent to 100 per cent of their time on environmental stories. And in Mountain West, 31 per cent said that they spend 67 per cent to 100 per cent of their time on environmental stories. In discussing barriers to reporting, reporters cited issues such as time constraints or the size of the news hole rather than interference by editors or advertisers.

Nevertheless, West *et al.*, (2001) in their study in October 1999, surveyed members of The Society of Environmental

Journalists working in radio, television, print media, government and academic settings. Journalists were asked about the extent to which factors such as scarcity of information, lack of editorial support, community misunderstanding and pressure from industry and environmental groups present challenges in covering environmental health issues. Community misunderstanding represented the greatest challenge journalists faced with regard to covering environmental issues. Half of the respondents identified it as a 'serious' challenge. One-third of the respondents identified lack of support by their editorial staff as a 'serious challenge' in covering environmental stories. Overall, more journalists (37%) felt that pressure from the industry represented a 'serious challenge' in covering environmental health issues compared with 20 per cent who described pressure from environmental groups as a 'serious challenge'.

In India, Sekhar (1981) researched the role of the press in promoting environmental concern in India. He concluded that for a number of reasons, the Indian press played only a limited role in creating mass concern about environmental issues. A content analysis conducted in 1979-80 revealed that a large number of environmental items were news reports; most stories were reactive, and there was very little evidence of investigative journalism. Mostly, environmental stories are not significantly covered in newspapers in India as compared to politics, crime or sports (Murthy, 2000). Normally, there are three types of environmental news available in the media. (1) environmental disaster news, (2) news about environmental activists or group actions and (3) environment-related scientific news (Suresh Kumar, A, undated). When there is an environmental disaster, newspapers cover the issue adequately for a considerable period of a week or two, and subsequently the news coverage declines until another disaster is noticed by the media. For instance, the tsunami of December 26, 2004 left a trail of destruction in the Asian region killing more than 150,000 people. The three southern states namely Andhra Pradesh, Tamilnadu and Kerala experienced the worst ever tragedy. Prompted by the tragedy, *The New Indian Express* deputed three reporters to investigate the reasons for huge losses suffered by the people. Moreover, the newspaper published five-part series of reports beginning from January 20, 2005 on the human greed which mismanaged ecology for many years (Murthy, 2006: 77). Secondly, environmental issues are focused in newspapers when environmental activists or groups campaign against an issue. For example, in 2003, the Perumatty Panchayat in Kerala decided not to renew the industrial license to Hindustan Coca Cola Beverages Ltd. on the grounds of "protecting public interest", as the company was "causing shortage of drinking water in the area through over-exploitation of ground water resources". Subsequently, the Kerala State Health Department confirmed the charges of depletion and contamination of well water in Plachimada village of Palakkad district. The issue was reported at the national level following rigorous follow-up by the regional press (Mazoomdar, 2006: 159). Third, scientific issues dealing with environment appear very scantily in newspapers in the inside pages or supplements (Vilanilam, 1993). The reasons for such kind of coverage of environmental issues are: *(i)* media's own aims and purpose, *(ii)* the ownership and control of media, *(iii)* media's perception of its audience, *(iv)* the environment issue's relation to other political and economical matters and *(v)* prejudice of the working media personnel (Suresh Kumar, A, undated). Further, Shourie (1995) pointed out that lack of specialization is a "running sore of Indian press—whether it is on defence or on power projects or on the size of dams or on the virtues or otherwise of atomic power, there are very few journalists who have worked at studying the subject in any detail."

Source Use

Research on media framing of environmental issues showed that sources did have a significant impact on news frames (Molotch and Lester, 1974; Liebler and Bendix, 1996). Moreover, mass communication research has generally found that reporters relied disproportionately on government officials as sources, resulting in a dominance of official perspectives (Taylor *et al.*, 2000; Sigal, 1986; Brown *et al.*, 1987). In environmental reporting, this source influence could be amplified by a tendency of reporters to rely on small set of sources (Friedman 1986, 1991) and to accept source statements uncritically (Dunwoody and Griffin, 1993). Sachsman *et al.*, (2004) found that majority of environment reporters more frequently framed their stories using government, human-interest, business, nature, pollution, politics, science, and health angles. Some reporters, ranging from 28.3 per cent in New England to 41.8 per cent in the Pacific Northwest, said that they rarely or never included risk assessment in their environmental stories. The study revealed that some reporters (16.9%-25.0%) generally had overblown environmental risks, unduly alarming the public. Further, Sachsman *et al.*, (2006) in another study found that environmental reporters spent much of their time covering non-environment stories. They relied more often on local and state sources than on national sources and used a variety of story frames and angles to construct their reporting.

In the USA, Lacy and Coulson (2000) analyzed newspaper coverage of six major metropolitan dailies to examine source use on the environmental beat. Major sources considered were government, business, consumer and environmental sources. The study found that reporters used government and business sources more extensively than consumer and environmental sources; source use would vary among newspapers in the study; source use would vary by reporter specialty; and source use would vary by origin of story. Similarly, Berkowitz and Beach (1993) observed that journalists used a greater variety of news sources for local stories than for those outside their metro areas. They noted that journalists develop a diverse pool of sources in their home communities and that when they went outside those communities, they were more dependent on obvious, high visibility sources. While analyzing the source use in Brazil, Reis study (1999) content-analyzed to determine the type of sources used as well as the kind of issues covered. The analysis showed that government officials were the most frequently cited sources, while environmentalists and scientists were all but ignored as news sources. The analysis also indicated that economic issues were surprisingly prominent in the coverage. Logan *et al.,* (2004) analyzed the coverage of public health crisis in two dailies in Korea from September 1999 to December 2000. The findings revealed that two Korean daily newspapers (*Chosun Ilbo* and *Hankyoreh*) emphasized governmental officials and physicians as news sources, underemphasized other news sources and limited in-depth reporting. However, the two newspapers used a range of sources and provided some multidimensional news coverage during the public health crisis. While both newspapers depended on governmental officials and physicians as news sources and provided less in-depth coverage, the overall findings did not reveal a pattern of journalistic neglect. Interestingly, Wilson (2000) analyzed reporters' understanding of climate change by identifying sources of reporter knowledge about climate change, measuring reporters' acquired knowledge against the scientific consensus and analyzing differences in reporter knowledge based on several factors that might influence climate change reporting. Results showed that reporters who primarily used scientists as sources and who worked in the environmental beat full-time had the most accurate climate change knowledge. Interestingly, an African study found that the majority of the environmental stories were having an urban source and the stories were written by urban writers when much of environmental issues took place in the rural settings (Aghan and Munuve, 2006).

News Coverage

A variety of authors with different perspectives attested to the importance of news media coverage in influencing knowledge levels, opinion and policy on environmental issues (Atwater *et al.,* 1985; Mazur and Lee, 1993; Ader, 1995; Davis, 1995; Hester and Gonzenbach, 1995). Both newspapers and television news played a demonstrable role in setting the agenda for environmental debate (Trumbo, 1996). A news report's frame was decided by the choices (attribution, phraseology, source selection, etc.) that present some facts as particularly salient (Entman, 1993; Pan and Kosicki, 1993;

Liebler and Bendix, 1996). In news coverage, climate change was widely reported as a scientific and environmental issue. In six months' news coverage of climate change in New Zealand, reporting of basic scientific facts was overwhelmingly accurate (Bell, 1994). Crawley (2007) analyzed agricultural biotechnology coverage appearing in a collection of community newspapers in Northern California and Missouri between 1992 and 2004. It examined the similarities and differences in news media frames used to focus the debate at the local level and evaluate the frequency and range of dominant political and social actors as news sources. Newspaper coverage in some community newspapers framed the story in more complex and diverse ways and included a wider range of voices than was reported in studies of coverage in the national elite press. Oppositional viewpoints existed in some local newspapers, perhaps more so in national news.

Another analysis showed that media was a key actor in the definition, articulation and popularization of environmental issues in Brazil. Environmental issues in the Brazilian press were constructed through a techno-centric perspective that stressed on traditional beliefs and values, emphasizing progress, technology, production and materialism. It also indicated that alternative environmental perspectives, which would criticize the core of industrialization and the status quo, did not receive the same amount of attention in the newspapers (Guedes, 2000).

In India, studies conducted in different settings found that environmental news coverage was very low. Vilanilam's analysis (1993) of 10 dailies (eight Malayalam and two English), during the period between June 1987 and May 1988 found that science and technology which also included environmental news occupied less than five per cent of the news hole. Preetha and Karippai's study (1996) of farm news in two Malayalam dailies in Kerala found that hardly 1.33 per cent of the news hole dealt with farm news. Srivastava's study (1996) of coverage of environmental news in four dailies in 1995 found that 0.7 per cent of the total print area was occupied by environmental issues. In another study, it was found that English and Telugu newspapers were giving less than one per cent of news hole to environmental news (Murthy, 2000).

Risk Communication

A large number of studies were conducted worldwide into risk communication following Three Mile Island and Chernobyl disaster (Gale, 1987; Rubin, 1987; Wilkins and Patterson, 1987). A number of studies suggested that the media generally failed to supply people with enough risk information. For example, a study by Friedman *et al.*, (1987) analyzed coverage in five newspapers and three main television networks in the USA over the two-week period following the Chernobyl accident. They concluded that television and newspapers did not provide enough space or explanation, to the effects of radiation upon health and the environment. A study conducted by Sandman *et al.*, (1987), focusing on environmental risk in the US press also came to similar conclusions. They found that very few of the articles that included a discussion of environmental risk addressed the amount of danger they posed. Friedman *et al.*, (1992) attempted to uncover whether enough background information about nuclear power and the nuclear industries in the USA, USSR and eastern and western Europe had been included during the first two weeks of US coverage of the Chernobyl accident so that Americans would not be misled in their understanding of and attitudes towards nuclear power in general. It also sought to determine if reporters took advantage of the Chernobyl accident to attack nuclear technology or the nuclear industry in general. Coverage was analyzed in five US newspapers and on the evening newscasts of the three major US television networks. Despite heavy coverage of the accident, not more than 25 per cent of the coverage was devoted to information on safety records, history of accidents and current status of nuclear industries. Not enough information was provided to help the public's level of understanding of nuclear power or to put the Chernobyl accident in context. However, articles and newscasts generally balanced the use of pro-nuclear and anti-nuclear statements and did not include excessive amounts of fear-inducing and negative information. A longitudinal content analysis study of German media coverage of the Chernobyl disaster by Merten *et al.,* (1990) found that the distribution of alarming and reassuring statements was about equal (Dunwoody and Peters, 1992). However, a review of Swedish research on Chernobyl coverage suggested that there was a much larger proportion of worrying compared with comforting statements in the Swedish media (Norhstedt, 1991).

Dudo *et al.,* (2007) analyzed four major US newspapers to assess the quality of coverage related to risks posed by avian flu. The quality of coverage was examined with a five-dimension conceptualization that included measures of risk magnitude, self-efficacy, risk comparisons, sensationalism, and thematic and episodic framing. Findings revealed that coverage was dominated by episodic frames, exhibited high sensationalism, and contained minimal information promoting self-efficacy. Conversely, coverage exhibited high quality in terms of risk magnitude and risk comparison information. Kitzinger and Reilly (1997) argued that source competition, journalists' training, 'newsworthiness', news momentum and the organization of news beats and media outlets encourage certain risks to be highlighted at particular times, but encourage other risk debates to be entirely overlooked.

Effective risk communication is central to good environmental risk management. While studies have shown that newspapers are the primary source of information to the public regarding environmental issues, little is known about how environmental news is used as a risk-communication tool. Wakefield and Elliott (2003) explored the role of local information systems in risk communication, using newspaper content analysis as well as in-depth interviews with journalists and community residents to develop a case study of an environmental assessment process for a non-hazardous industrial waste landfill. Results indicated that risk messages were chosen and shaped by journalists on the basis of their own exigencies. In addition, while newspapers were a major source of risk information, their impact was mitigated by resident distrust and access to other information sources, most notably their own personal information networks. These results had implications for environmental policy, as decision makers often use, either passively or actively, print media as a risk-communication tool. The emergence of West Nile virus in the US provided an opportunity to examine the effectiveness with which the print media communicated risks associated with a specific health threat. Roche and Muskavitch (2003) surveyed articles on West Nile virus published in major North American newspapers in the year 2000 to assess the efficacy of risk communication related to this disease. They found that articles generally presented risk information with a low degree of contextual precision, that is, information was generally more qualitative than quantitative and quantitative information that was present generally did not provide the relative context of a denominator. Therefore, the information provided was of limited usefulness to readers, in that it was insufficient to help readers to make personal decisions required to reduce overall personal risk while minimizing personal cost. Their findings suggested that there was a distinct need for the media to provide more precise information about health risks.

Contrary to the belief that the newspapers educate the public about the environmental risks, Major and Atwood study (2004) observed that environmental news tends to be dramatic and ambiguous with little information that helped the public understand the risks that existed in communities. This analysis was designed to identify differences between environmental news stories that reported risks with those that did not. The sample (N=841) news stories were drawn from 12,000 stories published between September 1, 1997 and August 31, 1998 in 93 Pennsylvania daily newspapers. Nearly 60 per cent of the news stories and releases did not mention risk. The findings suggested that the environmental issues and the environmental values supporting those issues predicted whether a news story would report risks. Sources, problem definitions, and traditional news values were less useful in differentiating risk from non-risk news stories and releases. The stories provided limited information that would facilitate public understanding of environmental risks.

Agenda-setting

The agenda-setting hypothesis has been influential in environmental communication research on the effects of mass media although different studies contradicted this hypothesis. One study, Iyengar and Kinder (1987) found firm evidence of the agenda-setting effect in their study of the evening news on television in which viewers rated the importance of environmental issues higher after viewing increased coverage of news of environmental pollution. Chan study (1999) tested the agenda-setting hypothesis for the environmental issue in Hong Kong from 1983 to 1995. It was found that the agenda-setting hypothesis was supported for the initial period of five and a half years. In the subsequent period of seven and a half years, despite the increased media coverage of the issues, there was a significant drop in the perceived salience of the environmental problem. This might be due to the dilution of public attention as a result of diversity in the news agenda and reporting of local environmental problems as 'soft' news. It was also found that the environmental issues failed to compete with other prominent issues directly affecting the public. The mass media played a much less important role in keeping the environmental issue on the public agenda at a later stage. Mikami *et al.,* (1995) examined how mass media in Japan influenced upon the public awareness of the global environmental issues during and prior to the Earth Summit (UNCED) in 1992. The survey revealed substantial public concern about environmental issues in Japan. Content analysis of television news during the UNCED, however, found relatively weak relationship between the salient environmental issues of the audience and portrayal of environmental issues in television news during the UNCED. An agenda-setting study of the newspapers during and before the UNCED showed a gradual and cumulative nature of the effects rather than the immediate effects. The amount of television viewing and the attitudes towards environmental tax showed positive association, after controlling for demographic variables which suggested cultivation effects of the media.

However, two studies observed that agenda-setting role of the media would not have an impact on the readers or audience. Suhonen (1993) found a negligible relation between the levels of environmental coverage in newspapers in Finland and levels of readers' concern about the environment. Gooch study (1996) of the coverage of environmental issues by Swedish newspapers did not find evidence of agenda-setting effect. Although reports about water pollution and waste received the greatest amount of news coverage in the press, the public rated other environmental concerns such as air quality as more serious.

Nevertheless, can the press set an agenda in environmental issues? Does the press build an agenda to highlight environmental issues? In some instances, the mass media can highlight the issues in mobilizing public opinion by setting an agenda. Shaw and McCombs (1989) commented that the "agenda-setting role of press is one of civic mobilization. The press helps focus our attention on the key problems of the day. It sets an agenda for action."

For instance, the Korean daily *Chosun Lo* launched an environmental campaign between 1992 and 1997 with the support of an environmental team. Opinion polls conducted a year after found that Korean's attitudes and behaviours were considerably influenced by the newspaper's coverage of environment (Park, 2001: 3). Thus, since the mass media is a part of modern life, environmental conflicts have increasingly become part of the public agenda and they now gain vast media coverage. While some studies agreed that the mass media sectors were essential for expanding and supporting democracy on global, national, and local levels alike, yet media's interference, by definition, escalated conflicts (Vraneski and Richter, 2002).

Perceptions of Journalists

Few journalists perceive environmental deterioration as a

problem that has to do with social values and life styles, to which technical solutions cannot be found out. Most journalists had a concern for the environment but they didn't consider themselves as 'green'. A study (Coulson and Lacy, 1996) was undertaken among 423 journalists who had worked in both competitive and single daily cities in the USA were asked their perceptions on how newspaper competition affects content. A majority of journalists said that competing dailies provided higher quality local news, a greater diversity of news, and a greater diversity of editorial opinions than non-competitive dailies. A majority also said that competing dailies were less likely to become complacent but more likely to sensationalize news. In the same survey, one-third of 1,667 journalists in single-daily cited said that broadcast news offered an acceptable local news alternative to the daily newspaper.

In Europe, Centre of Environmental Communication Studies (CEIA) conducted a survey among 25 European environmental communicators to ascertain the perceptions of journalists about environmental issues. The study found that majority of respondents perceived that environmental information transmitted by the media was insufficient. Above 18 per cent of the communicators believed that less coverage was due to the fact that environmental information was hard to understand by the population. Nevertheless, 14 per cent considered that the principal motive as the type of information was depressive. Another 14 per cent thought that the low presence of environmental information was a result of a higher concern from the part of media companies not to lose readers and audiences than to improve quality. 13 per cent of the journalists reported that though people consider environmental information of much interest, they were unable to do anything in this regard. 11 per cent of the environmental journalists considered that the basis of the problem was that many editors did not know enough about the topics they write about, and this generated general ignorance among the population on what they were able to do in relation to the environmental problem (Expert Corner Report, undated). The study also noted that one of the facts that could explain the public's difficulties in understanding environmental information relied on the communicators' general practice of using mainly governmental or official sources of information. Sources generally used by specialized journalists were institutional, while the scientific community had little prominence, and neither had industrial sectors or non-governmental organizations. Though newspapers were considered as the main environmental transmitters, they were at the same time perceived as the worst in terms of quality of this information. Nevertheless, several studies and surveys have demonstrated that they still received more credibility among citizens than they really deserved, given their insufficiencies and limitations.

In the UK, Hansen study (1994) observed that the newspaper coverage of science was governed and shaped by both macro-level factors such as ownership and cultural resonances and by the more micro-level factors of journalistic practices, professional values, and organizational arrangements. This study examined the characteristics and professional practices of specialist journalists involved in the coverage of science, medicine and related subjects in the British national press. It showed that they had shared many of their characteristics with specialist journalists in other areas: they valued journalistic professionalism and skill more highly than formal training in their particular field of specialist reporting; they deployed conventional news-value criteria, but emphasized in particular the importance of a 'relevance to the reader' criterion in the selection of science news; they deployed elaborate routines for securing the credibility of their reporting, including the active cultivation of a relationship of mutual trust with their sources, and a source-orientation which was distinctly institutionally- and authority-focused. Popular and quality press journalists held clearly different images of their target audiences, although for both categories of journalists the image of the readers owed more to journalistic judgment and casual feedback than to systematic readership data. The overriding key to understanding the work of these specialists was to recognize that they were, in their practices and professional beliefs, journalists first and specialists second.

Public Opinion

Media coverage of environmental issues informs the public and provides the basis for political mobilization. An underlying assumption of much of the research is that the media have powerful influence upon public attitudes to the environment. Frequently, researchers make the assumption that it is possible to demonstrate a direct causal relationship between media coverage and public opinion. Some studies suggest that the media have played an important role in influencing public opinion about environmental matters (Atwater *et al.,* 1985; Brosius and Kepplinger, 1990; Parlour and Schatzow, 1978; Salwen, 1988).

The mass media promote 'civil' discourse providing discussion of matters of dominant public concern (Hackett and Zhao, 1998). It is assumed that increased coverage corresponds to increased public awareness, and that "environmental meanings flow from certain sources through the media to the wider public" (Hansen, 1991; Love, 1990). When environmental pressure groups define news, they do so primarily through the forum of 'demonstration of public protest action' (Hansen, 1991: 450). While public protest over environmental issues might attract attention as a magnet to news coverage, it also suffered in credibility. News coverage in the print media is popularly understood as objective, independent of the issues it reports and exempt from political partisanship. For example, a German study by Brosius and Kepplinger (1990) found a relatively strong correlation between public and media agendas on energy supply issues. However, they noted that their findings should be treated with caution since agenda-setting timescales vary depending upon the category of issues. A more complex approach towards understanding the flow of information between the media and the public was found in ideology diffusion models of communication (Tichenor *et al.,* 1970). However these theories had to suffer from the basic limitations as described above.

Such studies portrayed the processes of mass communication as though they operated in a linear rather than an interactive fashion. In other words, they map the evolution of social problems in terms of clearly identifiable 'stages'. For example, Strodhoff *et al.*, (1985) viewed the diffusion of environmental information as starting with scientific claims makers, channeled through special interest magazines, then to magazines with a more general audience, through to the broader public. As Hansen noted, "in their pursuit of linearity, (such approaches) gloss over the interactive nature of meaning construction among and between institutions in society" (1991: 447). This tends to ignore the possibility that there might be considerable overlap between stages. Protess *et al.*, (1987) examined the public opinion and policy-making impact of a local television investigative series concerning the toxic waste disposal practices of a major Chicago University. In this case, the publication format was virtually identical to the earlier police brutality study: a multipart television report, aired during a "ratings sweeps" period, by the same correspondent on the same local television station. The series disclosed that the University of Chicago was storing potentially hazardous toxic chemical and radioactive wastes beneath several of its buildings, including some classrooms. Stories alleged that the storage violated Chicago Fire Department regulations, as well as the environmental standards of several states and federal agencies, including the US Environmental Protection Agency (EPA), the US Occupational Safety and Health Administration (OSHA), and the US Department of Energy. Each night the broadcast described an assortment of delays by the University in constructing relatively inexpensive facilities to ameliorate the waste disposal problem thus giving the investigative report its title "Wasted Time."

3
Research Methodology

Kerala is the first state in India to achieve the highest literacy level of its people. Because of the high literacy in the state, the political awareness among the people has led to widespread reading of newspapers, the highest newspaper consumption in the country (Franke and Chasin, 1992). Even the poor in the villages read about their demands and struggles in Malayalam magazines and newspapers. Further, the habit of newspaper reading has led to the formation of an authentic public opinion (Ramachandran, 1996: 206). Since newspaper reading is high in the state, it is expected to impact the readers when newspapers cover environmental issues adequately. As journalists are considered mass educators, their role in educating the masses is very important.

Research Questions

With this view, the present study attempted to find out the perceptions of journalists working in seven-broadsheet dailies located in four cities in Kerala viz., the *Malayala Manorama, Mathrubhumi, Deshabhimani, Kerala Kaumudi, Mangalam, The New Indian Express* and *The Hindu* on the environmental issues. From this point of view, the researcher proposed to ascertain answers to the following research questions.

1. Do newspapers in Kerala cover environmental issues adequately?

2. If so, can journalists play an effective role in covering environmental issues?
3. And, how do they perceive their role in newspaper organizations?
4. What can be the obstacles to them in covering environmental issues in Kerala?
5. What do they suggest to improve the coverage of environmental issues?

Objectives of Study

In view of the proposed research questions, the specific objectives formulated for the study are:

1. To examine the socio-demographic profile of journalists in the sample study;
2. To ascertain the professional obligations of the journalists with regard to coverage of environmental issues;
3. To find out journalists' perception of coverage of environmental issues by Kerala newspapers;
4. To ascertain journalists' perception of accountability while reporting on environment and how journalists rely on identifying sources for environmental reporting;
5. To examine the problems faced by journalists while covering environmental issues;
6. To analyze the coverage given to environmental issues by the select dailies in terms of frequencies of news items; and finally
7. To offer suggestions to improve the coverage of environmental issues and also reporting of these issues in Kerala dailies.

Keeping in view the objectives of the study, two research methods were used to collect data pertaining to the study: survey method to collect data from the respondents and content analysis to obtain data from the select dailies about the coverage of environmental issues in the four cities.

Survey Method

Research Setting

Kerala, located at the extreme southern tip of the Indian subcontinent has a landmass of 38,863 sq. km area (Figure 1). Geographically, it lies between the Arabian Sea to the west and the Western Ghats, identified as one of the world's biodiversity hotspots, to the east. The region has a tropical humid climate with a maximum daily temperature average of 36.7 °C and a minimum of 19.8 °C. Mean annual temperatures range from 25.0–27.5 °C in the coastal lowlands to 20.0–22.5 °C in the highlands. Department of Environment identified that Kerala has all the three maximally productive and biodiversity-wise richest ecosystems in the world, namely the tropical rainforest, the coastal freshwater and brackish water wetlands, and the coastal marine coral reefs compressed within a width of 50 km (www.indiatogether.org). The state has high rainfall spread over more than six months, bio-geographic position and long history of biological as well as human civilization

Figure 1: Map of India Showing Kerala

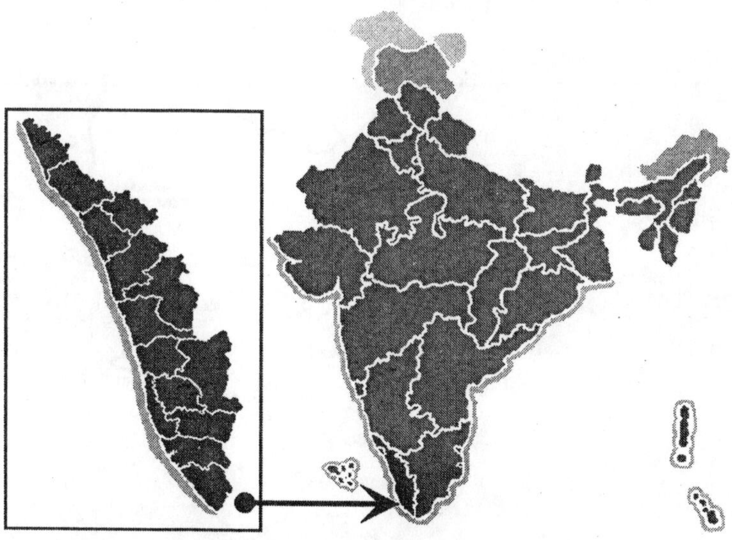

Source: www.Mapsofindia.com

continuity without major upheavals. Eastern Kerala consists of high mountains, gorges and deep-cut valleys whereas its western coastal belt is relatively flat, and are criss-crossed by a network of interconnected brackish canals, lakes, estuaries, and rivers.

Even when the state has the highest literacy rates in India, 94 per cent for men and 86 per cent for women, according to the 2001 census and the highest newspaper-consumption per capita of any place in India, it is subjected to various environmental problems. The urban environment is highly unhygienic with stagnated and contaminated water bodies, accumulation of degradable discards and litter, poor drains, polluted air and high level of noise. The tourism locations are fast deteriorating with litter, disposables and improper waste management (www.cleankerala.org).

Figure 2: Map of Kerala Showing all the Districts Including the Four Selected Cities

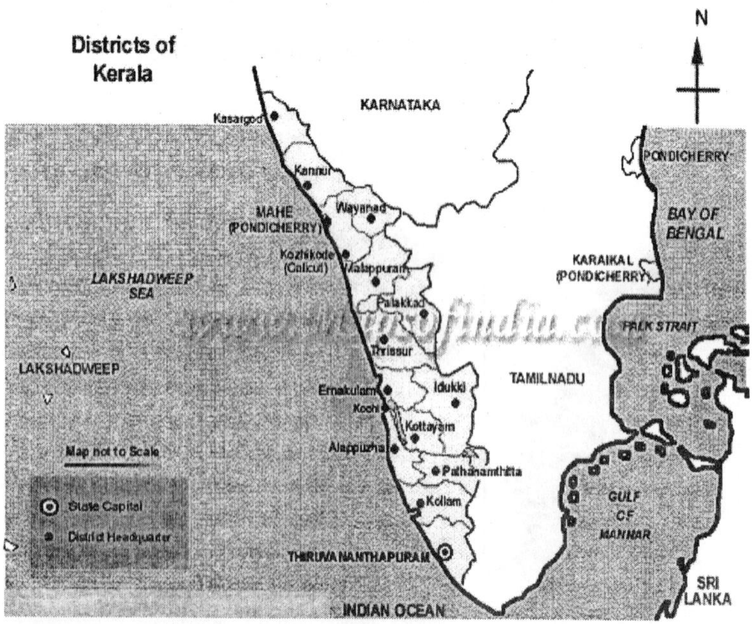

Source: www.Mapsofindia.com

The total sanitation programmes in Kerala are on a low key compared to the progress recorded in the human and social development. According to national sample survey (1991), out of 5.5 million households in Kerala, 2.9 million households are without individual sanitary latrines. (www.jalanidhi.com/health.htm) In rural and semi-urban areas, crops have been damaged and forest and aquatic ecosystems have been affected. Depleting water resources, changing land use patterns, denudation of forests, river sand mining, irrigation and power projects, use of chemical fertilizers and pesticides, mindless urbanization are other major concerns (Appendix II). There is an increasing population, reduction in space for habitation, developmental projects resulting in ecological degradation, changing life styles and an ever-increasing demand for luxury. In summer, the region is prone to gale force winds, storm surges, cyclone-related torrential downpours, occasional droughts, rise in sea level and storm activity.

The research setting for the present study is four cities viz., Thiruvananthapuram Kottayam, Kochi, and Kozhikode in Kerala (Figure 2). A brief media profile of the four selected cities is given below.

Thiruvananthapuram

The city has two English newspapers with their editions—*The New Indian Express* and *The Hindu* and six major Malayalam newspapers—*Mathrubhumi, Malayala Manorama, Kerala Kaumudi, Desabhimani, Madhyamam* and *Mangalam* are published from this place. Most Malayalam TV channels are based in Thiruvananthapuram. The government owned Doordarshan began broadcasting from here in 1981. Asianet, the first private Malayalam TV channel began operations in 1991. The other TV channels now based in Thiruvananthapuram are Surya TV, Amrita TV, Kairali TV, Kiran TV (youth channel of Surya TV), Asianet Plus (youth channel of Asianet) and People (news and current affairs channel of Kairali TV). The local cable services are provided by Asianet Satellite Communications Limited (Cable TV services wing of Asianet) and Siti Cable and they provide a number of local channels in addition to all the Indian TV channels. DTH services are available through Doordarshan Direct Plus and Dish TV. All India Radio has an AM (1161 MHz) and an FM (101.9 MHz) station for the city. The first private FM channel, "Radio DC" has commenced operations recently. There are over 20 cinemas and two movie studios in the city, Chithranjali and Merryland. The Kinfra Film and Video Park in the city has one of the most advanced film and animation production facilities in India.

Kottayam

Is the first town in India to have achieved hundred per cent literacy and is the publication centre of newspapers and periodicals. Four major dailies—*Malayala Manorama, Mathrubhumi, Deepika, Deshabhimani, Kerala Kaumudi* and *Mangalam* are being published from here. In the history of journalism, Kottayam occupies a prominent place. The origin of journalistic activity in the district can be traced back to the middle of the 19th century. *Jnananikshepam* (1848), *Vidyasamgraham* (1864), *Sandishtavadi* (1867) and *Malayala Mithram* (1878) were the early newspapers. *Nasrani Deepika,* which was started in 1887, later became the *Deepika*. K.C. Mammen Mapila started the *Malayala Manorama,* the largest circulated daily in India, at Kottayam in 1890. He also started *Bhashaposhini,* the literary magazine, in 1892.

Kochi

Major Malayalam newspapers are published in Kochi which include *Malayala Manorama, Mathrubhumi, Deshabhimani, Kerala Kaumudi, Mangalam* and *Deepika,* and English newspapers that include *The Hindu, The New Indian Express, Times of India* and *The Pioneer*. A number of evening papers are also published from the city. Newspapers in other regional languages like Hindi, Kannada, Tamil and Telugu have considerable circulation. Being the seat of the Kochi Stock Exchange, a number of financial publications are also published in the city—*The Economic Times, The Business Standard,* and *The Financial Times.* Prominent magazines like *The Week* and *Vanitha* and religious publications like *Satya Deepam* are also published from the city. Television networks in Kochi include India Vision, Kairali TV, Jeevan TV, Amrita TV and Manorama News. Satellite television services are available through Doordarshan Direct Plus, Dish TV and Tata Sky. All India Radio has two FM stations in the city, while private satellite radios such as WorldSpace, are also available. There are over twenty cinemas that screen movies in Malayalam, Tamil, English and Hindi. A film festival, known as the Kochi International Film Festival is held in the city every year.

Kozhikode

The place occupies a prominent place in the history of Malayalam journalism. The origin of journalism in this district can be traced back to 1880. The *Kerala Pathrika* is likely to be the earliest newspaper published from Kozhikode. *Keralam, Kerala Sanchari* and *Bharath Vilasam* are among the other newspapers that were published from Kozhikode before 1893. The two leading Malayalam newspapers, *Malayala Manorama* and *Mathrubhoomi* bring out Kozhikode editions. *Mathrubhoomi* has its headquartes in Kozhikode.

Recently two more dailies, *Varthamanam* and *Tejas* started publication from here. One of the major national dailies in English, *The New Indian Express* has a Kozhikode edition. *The Hindu* also has its office in the city. Other major newspapers having Kozhikode editions are *Kerala Kaumudi* and *Deshabhimani* and *Mangalam* The Kozhikode station of All India Radio was commissioned on 14 May 1950. The city is also the home ground for a number of literary magazines like *Mathrubhumi Azchapathippu* and *Chilla*. Some technical magazines like *IT Lokam* are also published from Kozhikode.

Operational Definition

The operational definition of the working journalists in the present study has been adopted from the Working Journalist Act, 1955. The Act defines the working journalist as follows:

> Working journalist means a person whose principal avocation is that of a journalist and who is employed

as such in, or in relation to, any establishment for the production or publication of a newspaper, or in, or in relation to any news agency, or syndicate supplying material for publication in any newspaper and includes an editor, a reader-writer, news-editor, sub-editor, feature-writer, copy tester, reporter, correspondent, cartoonist, news photographer and proof reader.

However, cartoonist, news photographer, proof reader, copy tester and journalists from news agencies have been excluded from the universe of the present study.

Universe and the Sample

The universe of the study consisted of journalists working in seven broadsheet dailies viz., the *Malayala Manorama, Mathrubhumi, Deshabhimani, Kerala Kaumudi, Mangalam, The New Indian Express* and *The Hindu*, published from four cities- Thiruvananthapuram, Kottayam, Kochi, and Kozhikode (Table 4). The criterion for a journalist to be included in the sample was that he or she must have a minimum experience of five years.

In order to prepare the universe of the study, the researcher obtained data from the respective newspaper offices about the total number of journalists working in each newspaper. Once the total number of journalists working in each newspaper office was obtained, the names of journalists were arranged in alphabetical order for each city to prepare the lists. More than 30 per cent of the journalists were randomly selected from seven newspapers in each city. Out of the total universe of 466 journalists, a total of 178 journalists were administered the questionnaire keeping in view the non-response and invalid questionnaires.

Out of 178 questionnaires, 16 questionnaires were found to be invalid. A total of 162 questionnaires remained for final analysis. Circulation figures and publication centres of the seven selected newspapers are given in Table 5.

Table-4
Distribution of Respondents in Four Cities by Newspapers

Newspapers	*City*			
	Thiruvananthapuram	*Kottayam*	*Kochi*	*Kozhikode*
Malayala Manorama	6	16	8	5
Mathrubhumi	7	6	4	8
Deshabhimani	7	5	6	5
Kerala Kaumudi	11	5	3	2
Mangalam	4	5	3	5
The New Indian Express	4	1	9	4
The Hindu	10	1	9	3
Total	49	39	42	32

N=162

Table-5
Circulation Figures of Sample Newspapers

Newspaper	*Average Net Paid Circulation*
Malayala Manorama	1,395,191
Mathrubhumi	1,040,183
Deshabhimani	227,214
Kerala Kaumudi	Not available
Mangalam	136,610
The New Indian Express	255,167
The Hindu	1,181,500

Source: Audit Bureau of Circulation Report, December 31, 2005.

Data Collection Instrument

Data collection instrument was a structured questionnaire, which included close-ended and open-ended questions relevant to the study. Part I of the questionnaire dealt with the identification data of respondents such as age, gender, education, income, working experience and so on. Part II contained questions relevant to professional obligations such as details of the profession, environmental reporting, sources of information, type of risks involved in environmental reporting and so on. Part III consisted of questions relating to newspaper coverage of environmental issues such as quality of environmental reporting, training for journalists and so on. Part IV included questions dealing with perception of journalists on specific environmental issues, role of newspapers in environmental issues and so on (Appendix III).

Pilot Study

The questionnaire thus prepared was pilot-tested among 10 per cent of the sample. The questionnaire was given to six journalists working in English newspapers and 12 in Malayalam newspapers. After the pilot study, the questionnaire was modified by incorporating few questions related to professional obligations, risks in the profession etc.

Data Collection Procedure

The data pertaining to the study were collected between September and December 2006. The researcher visited the newspaper offices and requested the respondents to fill the structured questionnaire at their convenience. As the researcher is a native of Kerala, contacts have been established with the respondents, who in turn introduced the researcher to other respondents. The researcher met the respondents in their offices for administering the questionnaire, and introduced herself as a former journalist resulting in obtaining cooperation from the respondent. The researcher waited in the respective newspaper office as the respondent filled the questionnaire and sometimes the researcher explained the purpose of the study during certain occasions. It took nearly half an hour to one hour for the respondent to fill the questionnaire.

Data Collection Problems

One main problem the researcher faced during data collection was the difficulty in meeting journalists. Even with prior appointments in the morning, reporters' schedule used to change due to unexpected events. The researchers had to meet them in the evening after they filed the reports, and were free from the work. Sub-editors were available only in the evening. By the time sub-editors arrived, it was time for them to begin the work. To meet the sub-editors, the researcher had to wait in the newspaper office till midnight. Some of them were available when their pages were signed off. Senior sub-editors filled the questionnaires after the pages for the first editions were signed off. Initially, some of the journalists were reluctant to fill the questionnaire, and when they were explained the purpose of the study, they co-operated with the researcher.

Because of these problems, the researcher had to repeatedly visit the newspaper offices. Some journalists were found to be on leave and this was a major problem for the researcher. In the beginning, the researcher requested the senior editors to permit her to meet the junior editors.

As the researcher approached the respondents through contacts, they wanted the questionnaire to be left with them. When the questionnaire was given to them and the researcher met them even after three or four days, the questionnaire was not filled. On some occasions, they misplaced the questionnaire. Therefore, researcher convinced the respondent that he or she could take enough of time, as the researcher could wait. Every time the educational background and professional experience of the researcher helped in convincing the respondents to fill the questionnaire.

Content Analysis of Select Newspapers

In order to examine the news contents of the seven selected dailies, content analysis was used as a research method. When the data were collected from the respondents between September and December 2006, the news contents of the environmental issues of the seven dailies of the same period were content analyzed to ascertain how the selected newspapers covered environmental issues. For the purpose of the analysis, the following procedure was used.

The Universe and the Sample

The universe of the study comprises seven selected dailies published from the four selected cities during the period between September 1 and December 31, 2006.

Sampling Procedure

While selecting the sample, it was thought that a sample of 10 per cent would be sufficient. This sample selected randomly would be adequate for generalizing to the universe (Riffe *et al.*, 1993). Two methods were adopted to select the editions of the newspapers to constitute the sample: 1. Continuous week and 2. Constructed week.

Stage One

A continuous week sampling method was adopted to select randomly one week from the four-month period, September, October, November and December 2006. Therefore, seven editions of each daily newspaper from each city were selected from September 1 to December 31, 2006.

Total number of days: 7

Total number of editions of each newspaper:
7 × 7 = 49 (7 days × 7 editions of each newspaper)

Total number of editions from each city
= 49 × 4 cities = 196 - 21 = 175

Since *The Hindu* is not published from two cities—Kottayam and Kozhikode and *The New Indian Express* from one city—Kottayam, the total number of editions that come under the continuous week sampling were 175.

Stage Two

The second stage comprised of a constructed week method

(Budd *et al.*, 1967). For this purpose, seven days of the week were randomly selected from the four month period to construct a week. That means a Monday, a Tuesday, a Wednesday, a Thursday, a Friday, a Saturday and a Sunday were randomly selected from all Mondays, Tuesdays, Wednesdays etc. The following days figured in the second stage sample—September 13, September 30, October 8, October 30, November 17, November 28 and December 7, 2006.

Total number of days: 7; Total number of editions: 7 × 7 = 49

Total number of editions from each city = 49 × 4 cities = 196 - 21 = 175

Overall 175 newspapers as two newspapers *The Hindu* and *The New Indian Express* were not published from Kottayam, Kozhikode and respectively (Table 6).

Table–6
Number of Editions Analyzed from Each City

Newspapers	*City*			
	Thiruvanantha-puram	*Kottayam*	*Kochi*	*Kozhikode*
Malayala Manorama	14	14	14	14
Mathrubhumi	14	14	14	14
Deshabhimani	14	14	14	14
Kerala Kaumudi	14	14	14	14
Mangalam	14	14	14	14
The New Indian Express	14	-	14	14
The Hindu	14	-	14	-
Total	98	70	98	84

N=14

Unit of Analysis

The unit of analysis of the study was a news item. The following items were excluded from the study sample: cartoons, editorials, letter-to-editor, illustrations, special supplements, Sunday magazines, book and film reviews, edit page articles, comics and stock-market quotations.

Operational Definitions

News Item

A news item was operationally defined as any item on a timely event with a current dateline, an account of that event reported by the paper's own correspondent, or staff reporter. However, news item includes news features also.

Environmental News

Environmental news was defined as any news item, according to the above criteria, focusing on environmental degradation and conservation, river pollution, industrial pollution, automobile pollution, and so on, preservation of forests, promotion of ecological awareness and court proceedings dealing with environmental issues.

Subject Categories

Two subject categories were developed for the purpose of coding: environment and other categories. The other items include all the news items excluding environment related news. In the environment related news items, the following subject categories were used for the study:

1. *Environment education:* Awareness campaigns, seminars, civic initiatives, protests, exhibitions, initiatives by schools and colleges, human interest stories (For example, an individual's initiative to clean the roads for highlighting the importance of sanitation).
2. *Climate change:* Global warming, pollution smog, international conferences and debates, change in rainfall, variation in temperatures.

3. *Sand mining:* Mining in hills, quarry mining, clay mining.
4. *Agriculture:* Forest resources, destruction of paddy fields and trees, spraying of pesticides, forest fires.
5. *Solid and hazardous waste disposal*: Biomedical, chemical, plastic, organic and inorganic waste.
6. *Drinking water/drinking water pollution:* Depletion of ground water, lack of water, leakage of drainage into drinking water sources.
7. *River pollution:* Letting out industrial effluents into the river.
8. *Government initiative:* Policy decisions, amendment of laws, court news.

Data Coding Sheet

A code sheet was prepared incorporating the subject categories mentioned above. The code sheet was pilot-tested by the researcher on 10 editions of the seven sample newspapers along with a second trained coder. Necessary changes were made to the subject categories based on the pre-test and the code sheet was finalized. All the news items were coded in terms of frequencies.

Inter-coder Reliability

Inter-coder reliability was calculated for unit of analysis under each subject category. After the first coder (researcher) completed coding all the subject categories, the second coder coded all the subject categories. When the totals of news items were available, Holsti formula (North *et al.*, 1963) was applied to calculate reliability. The inter-coder reliability for each subject category ranged from 90 per cent to 100 per cent. The Holsti formula was: $2(c_1, c_2)/\ c_1 + c_2$ where c_1 is the total number of items coded by first coder while c_2 is the total number of items coded by the second coder.

Data Reduction and Analysis

The data thus collected were analyzed using SPSS package to find out the relations between variables in survey and content analysis. Appropriate statistical tests were used to examine the significance between different variables.

4
Profile of the Print Journalist

The objective of this chapter is to present the profile of the print journalist who figured in the sample.

Characteristics

Out of 162 respondents who figured in the sample, a majority (21.6%) belonged to *Malayala Manorama* followed by *Mathrubhumi* (15.5%), *The Hindu* (14.1%) and *Deshabhimani* (14.1%). As much as 13 per cent belonged to *Kerala Kaumudi* and 11.2 per cent to *The New Indian Express* and 10.5 per cent to *Mangalam* daily (Table 7).

Table-7
Distribution of Respondents by Sample Newspaper

S.No.	*Newspaper*	*f*	%
1.	Malayala Manorama	35	21.6
2.	Mathrubhumi	25	15.5
3.	The Hindu	23	14.1
4.	Deshabhimani	23	14.1
5.	Kerala Kaumudi	21	13.0
6.	The New Indian Express	18	11.2
7.	Mangalam	17	10.5
	Total	162	100

Table 8 shows the distribution of respondents in selected cities—Thiruvananthapuram, Kochi, Kottayam and Kozhikode. Majority (30.2%) of the respondents are from Thiruvananthapuram followed by Kochi (25.9%), Kottayam (24.1%) and Kozhikode (19.8%).

Table–8
Distribution of Respondents in Selected Cities

S.No.	*City*	*f*	*%*
1.	Thiruvananthapuram	49	30.2
2.	Kochi	42	25.9
3.	Kottayam	39	24.1
4.	Kozhikode	32	19.8
	Total	162	100

Table 9 shows the percentage distribution of respondents in four cities by sample newspapers. Out of the 30.2 per cent respondents of *Malayala Manorama,* nearly 10 per cent are from Kottayam and 5 per cent from Kochi. *Mathrubhumi* was represented by nearly 5 per cent from Kozhikode and 4.3 per cent from Thiruvananthapuram. *Deshabhimani* had 4.3 per cent from Thiruvananthapuram and 3.7 per cent from Kochi. *Kerala Kaumudi* was represented by 6.8 per cent from Thiruvananthapuram and 2.5 per cent from Kottayam. *Mangalam* was represented by 3.7 per cent from Kottayam and 3.1 per cent from Kozhikode. 5.5 per cent of *The New Indian Express* was from Kochi and 2.5 per cent from Kozhikode. *The Hindu* was represented by 6.2 per cent from Thiruvananthapuram and 5.5 per cent from Kochi.

Designation

Table 10 shows the designation of the respondents by their designation. More sub-editors figured in the sample from *Malayala Manorama* (14.3%) and *Kerala Kaumudi* (7%) as compared to editors and reporters from other dailies. While more reporters figured in the sample from *The Hindu* (9.3%)

and *Mathrubhumi* (6.8%). However, more editors figured in the sample from *Mangalam* (3%).

Table–9
Percentage Distribution of Respondents in Four Cities by Sample Newspapers

Newspapers	*City*			
	Thiruvanantha-puram	*Kottayam*	*Kochi*	*Kozhikode*
Malayala Manorama	3.7	9.9	4.9	3.1
Mathrubhumi	4.3	3.7	2.5	4.9
Deshabhimani	4.3	3.1	3.7	3.1
Kerala Kaumudi	6.8	2.5	1.9	1.2
Mangalam	2.4	3.7	1.9	3.1
The New Indian Express	2.4	0.6	5.5	2.5
The Hindu	6.2	0.6	5.5	1.9
Total	30.2	24.1	25.9	19.8

N=162

Table–10
Percentage Distribution of Respondents by their Designation

	Newspaper						
Designation	*Malayala Manorama (n=35)*	*Mathru-bhumi (n=25)*	*Deshabhi-mani (n=23)*	*Kerala Kaumudi (n=21)*	*Mangalam (n=17)*	*The New Indian Express (n=18)*	*The Hindu (n=23)*
Editors	1.2	2.4	1.2	1.8	3.0	0.6	1.2
Reporters	6.1	6.8	6.1	4.2	3.1	6.2	9.3
Sub-editors	14.3	6.3	6.8	7.0	4.4	4.3	3.7
Total	21.6	15.5	14.1	13.0	10.5	11.1	14.2

N=162

Gender

In respect of gender, majority (90.1%) were male journalists (Table 11) while the remaining were female journalists (9.9%). Out of the 16 female journalists in the sample, majority were from *The Hindu* (5), followed by *Malayala Manorama* (4), *The New Indian Express* (3) and two each from *Mathrubhumi* and *Deshabhimani*.

Table–11
Percentage Distribution of Respondents by Gender

S.No.	*City*	*f*	%
1.	Male	146	90.1
2.	Female	16	9.9
	Total	162	100

Age

Table 12 shows the age group of respondents in the sample. Most (31.5%) of the respondents belonged to the age group of 35-39 years. The group included *Malayala Manorama* (8.6%), *Mathrubhumi* (4.3%), *Deshabhimani* (6.2%), *Kerala Kaumudi* (4.9%) and *The New Indian Express* (3.7%). Followed by this group, about 21 per cent were in the age group of 40-44. But in the age group of 25-29 (8%), most of the respondents belonged to *Mangalam*. Three respondents belonged to the age group of 54-59 years and they were from *Mathrubhumi*. In the sample, the minimum age was 27 years and the maximum age was 59 years. The mean age of the respondent was 39 years.

Education

Regarding the level of education of respondents, majority (80.9%) were post-graduates followed by post-graduate diploma holders (9.8%) and graduates (8.1%), 1.2 per cent respondents were Ph.D. holders in Malayalam literature, and they were one each from *Mathrubhumi* and *Deshabhimani*. All the other respondents hold diploma in Journalism and Mass Communication (Table 13).

Table-12
Percentage Distribution of Respondents by Age

Age	*f*	%
25-29	13	8.0
30-34	29	17.9
35-39	51	31.5
40-44	34	20.9
45-49	17	10.6
50-54	15	9.2
54-59	3	1.9
Total	162	100

$\overline{X} = 39$ years

Table-13
Percentage Distribution of Respondents by Level of Education

Level of Education	*f*	%
Ph.D.	2	1.2
Postgraduate	131	80.9
P.G. Diploma	16	9.8
Graduate	13	8.1
Total	162	100

Income

In terms of income, 32.7 per cent of the respondents were in the income group of 100,000-150,000, followed by the income group of 150,001-200,000 at 22.9 per cent. In the study sample, maximum income per annum was Rs. 400,000 and minimum income per annum was Rs. 50,000. Only 18.5 per cent of the respondents had income per annum ranging between

Rs. 50,000-100,000. Nine respondents reported their annual income to be above Rs. 300,001. The mean income of the respondent per annum was Rs. 178,129 (Table 14).

Table–14
Percentage Distribution of Respondents by Level of Income Per annum

Income Range (In Rupees)	*f*	%
50,000-100,000	30	18.5
100,001-150,000	53	32.7
150,001-200,000	37	22.9
200,001-250,000	19	11.7
250,001-300,000	14	8.6
300,001 and above	9	5.6
Total	162	100

$\overline{X}$ = Rs. 1,78,129

Table–15
Percentage Distribution of Respondents by Duration of Service

Duration of Service (In Years)	*f*	%
5-9	42	25.9
10-14	56	34.7
15-19	25	15.4
20-24	25	15.4
25-29	10	6.2
30-34	2	1.2
35-39	2	1.2
Total	162	100

Duration of Service

Out of the 162 respondents, 34.7 per cent have 10-14 years of service, while 25.9 per cent of them have less than 9 years (Table 15). The criteria adopted for duration of service to be included in the sample was five years, and therefore journalists figured in the sample were having five or more years of service. Four respondents in the sample had more than 30 years of experience out of which one was from *The Hindu* and three were from *Mathrubhumi.*

About 6 per cent of the respondents from *Mathrubhumi* had 20-24 years of service while 10 per cent of the respondents from *Malayala Manorama* had 10-14 years of service. In *The Hindu,* 3.1 per cent of the respondents had 20-24 years of service. However, 6.2 per cent of the respondents each from *Mangalam* and *The New Indian Express* had 5-9 years of service. In the sample, maximum duration of service was 36 years and minimum duration was 5 years and mean duration of service was found to be 14.4 years.

Job Satisfaction

Satisfaction of the job is one criterion for efficient work. Comfortable salary, good working environment, job security etc. can be the major factors determining the job satisfaction. Are journalists in Kerala newspapers satisfied with their job, what are their perceptions about reasons for job satisfaction? To ascertain the reasons for job satisfaction of the respondents, an attempt was made in the present study.

Out of the 162 respondents, 88.2 per cent respondents reported that they were satisfied with the employment while 3.7 per cent were not satisfied and 8.1 per cent reported that they couldn't say anything about the job. Table 16 shows the newspaper-wise distribution of satisfaction of the respondents in the sample. Out of the 162 respondents in the sample, 97.1 per cent from *Malayala Manorama* opined that they were satisfied with job, followed by *Mathrubhumi* (92%). From the two English dailies, 86.9 per cent from *The Hindu* reported that they were satisfied with their job. 23.5 per cent respondents of *Mangalam* and 13.1 per cent from *The Hindu* said that they couldn't say whether they are satisfied or not.

Table–16
Are You Satisfied with the Job?

	Newspaper						
Satisfied with the Job	*Malayala Manorama (n=35)*	*Mathru-bhumi (n=25)*	*Deshabhi-mani (n=23)*	*Kerala Kaumudi (n=21)*	*Mangalam (n=17)*	*The New Indian Express (n=18)*	*The Hindu (n=23)*
Yes	97.1	92	91.3	85.7	70.6	83.3	86.9
No	2.9	4	8.7	-	5.9	5.6	-
Can't say	-	4	-	14.3	23.5	11.1	13.1
Total	100	100	100	100	100	100	100

N=162 X^2=16.89 df=12 ns

Job satisfaction was measured on a four-point scale: Very good, good, bad, very bad. Out of the 149 respondents who said that they were satisfied, a majority (65.7%) reported that their job satisfaction level was good followed by 34.3 per cent respondents who said that job satisfaction level was very good. Out of the six respondents who said that they were not satisfied, four of them reported that their job satisfaction level was bad followed by two respondents who reported that job satisfaction level was very bad.

Out of 143 respondents who reported very good and good for job satisfaction, 76.5 per cent from *Malayala Manorama* reported good, followed by 71.4 per cent from *Deshabhimani,* 66.7 per cent each from *Mangalam* and *The New Indian Express* and 61.1 per cent from *Kerala Kaumudi.* From *The Hindu,* 60 per cent of the respondents said that their job satisfaction was good followed by 52.2 per cent from *Mathrubhumi.* However, 47.8 per cent from *Mathrubhumi* reported very good for job satisfaction followed by *The Hindu* (40%) and *Kerala Kaumudi* (38.9%) (Table 17). 33.3 per cent of the respondents each from

Table–17
Job Satisfaction Levels: Newspaper-wise Distribution of Respondents

	Newspaper						
Opinion	*Malayala Manorama (n=34)*	*Mathru-bhumi (n=23)*	*Deshabhi-mani (n=21)*	*Kerala Kaumudi (n=18)*	*Mangalam (n=12)*	*The New Indian Express (n=15)*	*The Hindu (n=20)*
Very Good	23.5	47.8	28.6	38.9	33.3	33.3	40
Good	76.5	52.2	71.4	61.1	66.7	66.7	60
Total	100	100	100	100	100	100	100

.N=143

Mangalam and *The New Indian Express* said that job satisfaction was very good followed by 28.6 per cent from *Deshabhimani* and 23.5 per cent from *Malayala Manorama*. Out of the 6 respondents who mentioned that they were not satisfied with their job, five respondents belonged to the regional dailies and one to the English daily.

Table–18
Reasons for Job Satisfaction as Expressed by Respondents

Reason	*f*	%
Good working environment	91	63.6
Job security	27	18.9
Comfortable salary	12	8.4
Dealing with subjects of interest	6	4.2
Freedom at work	4	2.8
Political inclination	2	1.4
Organization's credibility	1	0.7
Total	143	100

When asked about the reasons for job satisfaction, respondents reported seven different reasons for their job satisfaction. Nearly 64 per cent of the respondents reported good working environment for job satisfaction whereas nearly 19 per cent of the respondents cited job security as their reason for job satisfaction (Table 18). 8.4 per cent of the respondents gave preference to comfortable salary whereas 4.2 per cent of the respondents opined that reporting subjects of interest is making them happy. While 2.8 per cent of the respondents sighted freedom at work as the reason for their satisfaction, negligible percentage of 0.7 per cent gave organization's credibility for job satisfaction. Interestingly, 1.4 per cent reported political inclination as the reason for their job satisfaction. The chi-square analysis showed significant differences for job satisfaction at $P > .1$ ($X^2 = 57.02$ df=36).

Out of the 143 respondents who reported that they were satisfied with their job, 80 per cent from *The New Indian Express*, 77.7 per cent from *Kerala Kaumudi*, 76.2 per cent from *Deshabhimani* and 75 per cent from *Mangalam* reported good working environment for job satisfaction (Table 19). However, 20 per cent from *The Hindu* and 17.7 per cent from *Malayala Manorama* gave comfortable salary as the reason for their satisfaction. 35.3 per cent from *Malayala Manorama,* 25 per cent from *The Hindu* and 21.7 per cent opined job security as the reason for their satisfaction with their job. However, 13.3 per cent of the respondents from *The New Indian Express* followed by 8.3 per cent from *Mangalam* found the chance to report subjects of interest as the reason for their satisfaction. Freedom at work is an essential criterion that can determine the satisfaction. Nearly 8 per cent of respondents from *Mathrubhumi* and *Mangalam* reported freedom at work as the reason whereas 9.6 per cent of the respondents from *Deshabhimani* reported political inclination as reason for their satisfaction. For 5 per cent of the respondents from *The Hindu,* organization's credibility was reason for satisfaction. Overall, the duration of service and job satisfaction showed a strong negative correlation ($r = -.65$).

Tablc-19
Job Satisfaction: Percentage Distribution of Respondents who Expressed Different Reasons

	Newspaper						
Reason	*Malayala Manorama (n=34)*	*Mathru-bhumi (n=23)*	*Deshabhi-mani (n=21)*	*Kerala Kaumudi (n=18)*	*Mangalam (n=12)*	*The New Indian Express (n=15)*	*The Hindu (n=20)*
Good working environment	44.1	65.2	76.2	77.7	75.1	80.0	50.0
Comfortable salary	17.7	4.4	4.8	-	-	-	20.0
Job security	35.3	21.7	4.8	16.8	8.3	-	25.0
Dealing with subjects of interest	2.9	-	4.8	5.5	8.3	13.3	-
Freedom at work	-	8.7	-	-	8.3	6.7	-
Political inclination	-	-	9.6	-	-	-	-
Organi-zation's credibility	-	-	-	-	-	-	5.0
Total (%)	100	100	100	100	100	100	100

N=143 X^2= 57.82 df=36 P >.10 significant

Out of the six respondents who were not satisfied with their employment, three of them (50%) cited lack of job satisfaction as the reason (Table 20). Others gave low salary, lack of support of management and lack of other opportunities as reasons.

Table–20
Lack of Job Satisfaction:
Reasons Cited by Respondents

Reason	*f*	%
Low salary	1	16.7
Lack of support of management	1	16.7
Lack of other opportunities	1	16.7
Lack of job satisfaction	3	50.0
Total	6	100*

* The percentage has been rounded off to 100.

5

Environment, Print Journalists and Professional Obligations

Like any other profession, journalism too has obligations related to the profession. Since, the newspapers serve the people with information needs; they act with responsibility in discharging their functions. However, journalists too have their own priorities in their profession, and hence an attempt is made to ascertain their views on their professional responsibilities as well as their role in society.

Journalism as a Profession

By disseminating information, journalism makes a citizen well-informed. In this regard, out of 162 respondents in the sample, a majority of 95.7 per cent believed that profession of journalism could help the society. However, 4.3 per cent was not sure about it.

Table–21
Respondents' Perception of the Journalism Profession

S. No.	*Perception*	*% (n=155)*
1.	It can create awareness among readers	47.7
2.	It can support peoples' cause	43.9
3.	It can make Government act	8.4
	Total	100

How could the profession be helpful to society? 47.7 per cent have reported that it can be used to create awareness among readers while 43.9 per cent reported that it could support peoples' cause (Table 21). 8.4 per cent of the respondents expressed the view that it can make Government act on issues of concern.

Accountability

Pritchard (1991, 2000) defined press accountability as a process by which press organizations may be expected or obliged to render an account to their constituents. A constituent is an individual, group, or organization whose goodwill is important for any media organization. Moreover, a media organization can have many constituents including audience members, advertisers, news sources, peers in other organizations and regulatory authorities. Further, the newspaper gathers information from various sources and disseminates it to the public. In the process, journalists are accused of violating the professional code of ethics (Murthy, 2005: 1). When asked whether the journalists are accountable while reporting on environment, out of the total 162 respondents in the sample, a majority of 83.9 per cent of the respondents said that journalists are accountable while reporting on environmental issues. However, 8.7 per cent of the respondents said that they are not accountable and a close 7.4 per cent said that they couldn't say anything about it.

Regarding the issue of accountability while reporting on environment, a majority of 90.4 per cent of the respondents reported that journalists are accountable to the newspaper readers whereas 6.7 per cent thought they are accountable to the newspaper management (Table 22). While 1.5 per cent respondents said they are accountable to their conscience, 0.7 per cent of the respondents said they were accountable to the environmental NGOs and 0.7 per cent of the respondents said they were accountable to the judiciary.

Frequency of Environmental Reporting

Newspapers like other channels inform the readers about environmental issues. What do journalists in Kerala think about

Table–22
To Whom are They Accountable?

Response	*% (n=136)*
Newspaper readers	90.4
Newspaper management	6.7
Environmental NGOs	0.7
To self-conscience	1.5
To judiciary	0.7
Total	100

the coverage of environmental issues in the newspapers? For this question, 66.7 per cent of the respondents believed that newspapers in Kerala report environmental issues frequently. Nevertheless, 30.8 per cent of the respondents disagreed with this view while 2.5 per cent could not say anything.

Table–23
Reason for Reporting Environmental Issues

Reason	*% (n=162)*
When an environmental issue surfaces	68.5
When there is an environmental conflict	29.1
Because of vested interests	1.2
Because of lack of stories	1.2
Total	100

"The environment doesn't make news when green initiatives are going forward; it makes news when they are being rolled back. That's because conflict makes news", says Andrew Tyndall, editor of the Tyndall report (cited in Rogers, 2002). When the respondents were asked to cite when environmental news appear in the Kerala newspapers, 68.5 per cent reported that they appear when an environmental issue surfaces. About 29 per cent said that environmental reports appear more when there is an environmental conflict

(Table 23). However, two (1.2%) of the respondents said that environmental news appears because of vested interests. Interestingly, two (1.2%) respondents said that they appear when there is a lack of stories to publish.

Newspaper-wise, 12.3 per cent respondents each from *Malayala Manorama* and *Mathrubhumi* felt that Kerala newspapers report environmental issues when an environmental issue surfaces followed by 10.5 per cent from *The Hindu*, 9.3 per cent from *Kerala Kaumudi*, 8.6 per cent from *Deshabhimani*, 8 per cent from *The New Indian Express* and 7.4 per cent from *Mangalam*. However, 8.6 per cent from *Malayala Manorama*, 4.3 per cent from *Deshabhimani* and 3.7 per cent each from *Kerala Kaumudi* and *The Hindu* opined that it's an environmental conflict that can make Kerala newspapers report environmental issues.

Reasons for Environmental Issues

As the world's population grows from six billion people in 2001 to an estimated nine billion in 2050 and development process gains pace, pressure on world's limited water, air, soil and other natural resources will only increase and environmental controversies are likely to grow. Hence environmental controversies are likely to grow as these pressures increase (Detjen, 2001: 17).

Therefore, in the present study, when the researcher asked a specific question about the main cause of environmental problems in Kerala, 48.8 per cent of the respondents cited man's indifference to environment as the reason while 30.9 per cent of the respondents reported lack of proper planning as the reason (Table 24 and Figure 3). Nearly 9 per cent of the respondents, however, gave industrialization as the reason while 2.4 per cent respondents cited political patronage and 1.2 per cent respondents felt lack of proper legal structure as the cause of environmental problems.

Newspaper-wise, majority of the respondents felt that man's indifference to environment is a major contributing factor to environmental issues. This response was given by 9.3 per cent

Table-24
Main Reason for Environmental Problems in Kerala as Perceived by the Respondents

Reason	%
Man's indifference to environment	48.8
Lack of proper planning	30.9
Industrialization	8.6
Lack of interest by government	8.1
Political patronage	2.4
Lack of proper legal structure	1.2
Total	100

from *Malayala Manorama,* 8.6 per cent each of the respondents from *Mathrubhumi, Deshabhimani* and *The Hindu* and 6.8 per cent from *Kerala Kaumudi.* 8.6 per cent of the respondents from *Malayala Manorama,* 5.6 per cent of respondents from *The New Indian Express* and 4.3 per cent of respondents from *Mangalam.* 2.5 per cent respondents from *Kerala Kaumudi* felt that lack of interest by Government is leading to environmental problems.

Figure 3: Main Reason for Environmental Problems in Kerala as Perceived by the Respondents

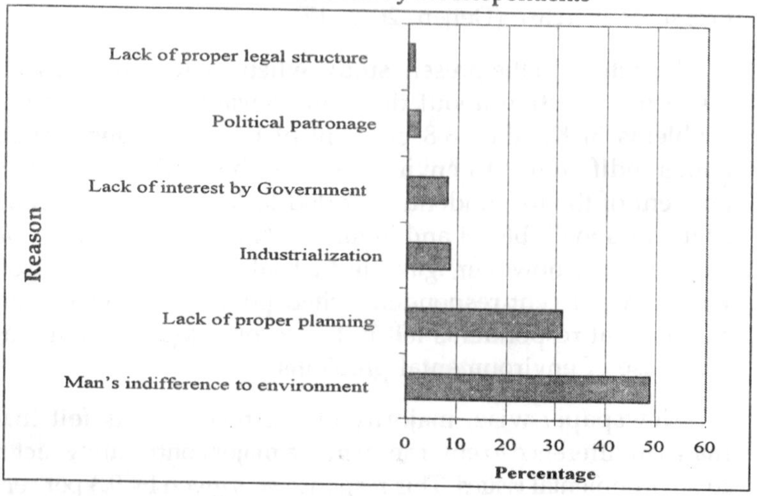

Need for Environmental Journalist

Can environmental reporting be improved by having a journalist exclusively on this beat? A majority (91.9%) of the total respondents felt that newspapers in Kerala require a journalist to be on environmental beat. About 7 per cent of the respondents stated that there need not be a journalist only on environmental beat.

Asked whether it is difficult to cover environment, about 65 per cent reported that environmental reporting is not difficult to cover while 28.4 per cent of the respondents agree that environmental coverage is difficult. Nearly 7 per cent of the respondents said they couldn't say whether it is difficult or not.

Frequency of Reporting by the Respondents

An attempt was made to assess the frequency of reporting of environmental issues by the respondents in the sample. It was measured on a three-point scale—less frequently, frequently and very frequently.

Table-25
Frequency of Reporting Environmental Issues by Respondents

Response	*% (n=107)*
Less frequently	53.3
Frequently	37.4
Very frequently	9.3
Total	100

Table 25 shows the frequency of reporting environmental issues by respondents. Out of the 107 respondents who have reported, only 9.3 per cent of the respondents reported very frequently followed by 37.4 per cent of the respondents who said that they had reported frequently and a close half of 53.3 per cent said that they had reported less frequently.

In terms of specific newspapers, 3.7 per cent of the respondents from *Mathrubhumi*, 1.9 per cent each from *Malayala Manorama* and *Deshabhimani* reported that they had covered report environmental issues very frequently. 8.4 per cent from *Kerala Kaumudi*, 6.5 per cent from *The Hindu*, 5.6 per cent from *Mangalam*, 4.7 per cent each from *Mathrubhumi* and *Deshabhimani* and 3.7 per cent each from *The New Indian Express* and *Malayala Manorama* said that they had reported environment issues frequently. However, 19.6 per cent of the respondents from *Malayala Manorama*, 8.4 per cent from *The Hindu*, 6.5 per cent from *Deshabhimani* and 3.7 per cent each from *Mathrubhumi* and *Mangalam* and 0.9 per cent from *Kerala Kaumudi* said they reported environment issues less frequently.

Table–26
Frequency of Reporting Environmental Issues: Year-wise

No. of News Stories	*2004-05*	*%*	*2005-06*	*%*
1-5	89	83.2	92	85.9
6-10	14	13.1	9	8.4
11-15	2	1.9	3	2.8
16 -20	2	1.9	3	2.8
Total	107		107	

Mean number of news items for 2004-05 = 4.12
Mean number of news items for 2005-06 = 4.12

Table 26 shows the frequency of reporting environmental issues by respondents during the year 2004-05 and 2005-06. Mean frequency in 2004-05 was found to be 4.12 and during 2005-06, it was also found to be 4.12.

Journalists' perception on why they have not been able to report was also ascertained. Among the 52 respondents who said that they had not reported environmental issues, 65.3 per cent of the respondents reported that there was a lack of opportunity to report whereas 21.2 per cent cited lack of time as the reason (Table 27). However, six respondents (11.6%)

said that they were unable to report though opportunity was there and one respondent (1.9%) reported that environmental issues were difficult to report.

Table–27
Reasons Cited by Respondents for not Reporting Environmental Issues

Reason	*% (n=52)*
Lack of opportunity to report	65.3
Lack of time to pursue issues	21.2
Unable to report though opportunity is there	11.6
Difficulty in understanding the subject	1.9
Total	100

In terms of specific newspapers 19.2 per cent from *Mathrubhumi* followed by 13.5 per cent from *Deshabhimani*, 9.6 per cent each from *Malayala Manorama* and *Kerala Kaumudi* reported lack of opportunity whereas 5.8 per cent each of the respondents from *Mangalam* viewed lack of opportunity as well as lack of time to pursue issues as the reason. About 8 per cent of the respondents from *The New Indian Express* also cited lack of time to pursue issues as the reason. Nearly 6 per cent of respondents from *The Hindu* found lack of opportunity as the reason and another 6 per cent reported that they were unable to report even though opportunity existed for them. One respondent from *Kerala Kaumudi* cited difficulty in understanding environmental issues as the reason. No respondent reported of any restriction from the management for not reporting.

What do the journalists in Kerala newspapers think about the environmental beat? Questions were asked to ascertain their perceptions on the environmental beat. Out of the 162 respondents, 81.5 per cent of the respondents obtained professional satisfaction by reporting environmental issues. However, 5.6 per cent said that they did not receive any satisfaction and 12.9 per cent said they couldn't say whether there was satisfaction in environmental reporting. However, 57.4 per cent of the respondents reported that they would receive better recognition by reporting on environmental issues while 12.4 per cent said that there was no better recognition.

Attitude Towards the Beat

Attitude of a journalist is an important factor in determining the quality of the news report. This is more so in the case of environmental beat as it is meant for a social cause to attain a better living environment. What are the factors that define interest or lack of interest in a journalist towards the beat? About 70 per cent of the total respondents found environmental reporting interesting while 8.6 per cent of the respondents found environmental reporting was not interesting.

Table–28
Reason for Showing Interest on Environmental Reporting

Reason	*% (n=110)*
The beat makes me feel socially responsible	22.7
The beat takes me closer to man and nature	21.8
Environment is related to everyday life	20.0
It is journalist's duty to report on people's cause	18.2
The beat gives me satisfaction and recognition	10.9
It is a less explored area	6.4
Total	100

Table 28 shows that out of the 110 respondents who found environmental reporting interesting, 22.7 per cent of the respondents reported that beat makes him or her socially responsible. 22 per cent cited the reason that the beat takes him or her closer to man and nature. For 20 per cent of the respondents, environment is related to everyday life and hence reporting on environmental issues is interesting. 18.2

per cent of the respondents related environmental reporting to people's cause. For 10.9 per cent of the respondents, the beat gives satisfaction and recognition and for 6.4 per cent of the respondents, the beat is interesting because it is a less explored area.

Table–29
Reason for Showing Interest on Environmental Reporting: Newspaper-wise

	Newspaper						
Reason	*Malayala Manorama (n=27)*	*Mathru-bhumi (n=15)*	*Deshabhi-mani (n=16)*	*Kerala Kaumudi (n=14)*	*Mangalam (n=9)*	*The New Indian Express (n=12)*	*The Hindu (n=17)*
Beat makes me socially responsible	33.3	-	18.7	28.6	11.1	16.6	17.6
Beat takes me closer to man and nature	29.6	40	25	14.3	-	25	17.6
Environment is related to everyday life	3.7	6.6	-	21.4	33.4	16.7	17.6
Beat helps to report on people's cause	7.4	26.7	18.7	14.3	22.2	25	23.6
Beat gives satisfaction and recognition	11.2	20	37.6	21.4	22.2	16.7	23.6
It is a less explored area	14.8	6.7	-	-	11.1	-	-
Total	100	100	100	100	100	100	100

X^2=35.24 df=30 P> .05 ns

Table 29 shows newspaper-wise distribution of respondents of reason for showing interest in environmental reporting. 33.3 per cent of the respondents from *Malayala Manorama,* 28.6 per cent from *Mathrubhumi,* 18.7 per cent from *Deshabhimani* and 17.6 per cent from *The Hindu* opined that the reason for showing interest in environmental reporting is that the beat makes him or her socially responsible. 40 per cent of the respondents from *Mathrubhumi* found the possibility of the beat taking him or her closer to man and nature as the reason for the interest followed by 29.6 per cent from *Malayala Manorama,* 25 per cent each from *Deshabhimani* and *The New Indian Express* and 17.6 per cent from *The Hindu.* For 33.4 per cent of the respondents from *Mangalam* and 21.4 per cent from *Kerala Kaumudi,* environment is related to everyday life. 26.7 per cent of the respondents from *Mathrubhumi* followed by 25 per cent from *The New Indian Express,* 23.6 per cent from *The Hindu* and 22.2 per cent from *Mangalam* thought that it was the duty of a journalist to report on people's cause. However, the chi-square analysis did not show significant differences among journalists in their perceptions of environmental reporting at $P > .05$ (X^2=35.24 df=30)

Table-30
Reason for not Showing Interest in Environmental Reporting

Reason	*% (n=14)*
Lack of knowledge on the subject	28.6
It has become artificial and self-centered	21.6
There are other issues more important	14.2
There is no glamour attached	14.2
It does not have news value	14.2
Political news reporting is more sought after	7.2
Total	100

Out of the 14 respondents who said that environmental reporting is not interesting, 28.6 per cent of the respondents reported lack of knowledge on the subject as the reason (Table 30). 21.6 per cent of the respondents stated that environmental reporting became artificial and self-centered. Two respondents from *Mangalam* cited that environment reporting had no news value and two respondents, one each from *Mangalam* and *Mathrubhumi* reported that there was no glamour attached to environment reporting. Two other respondents found that there are other issues that are more important. Interestingly, 7.2 per cent of the respondents said that political news items were more sought after by the readers in newspapers.

Special Qualities

Two persistent criticisms of environmental reporting are that journalists are not covering environmental science and that research covered by the media needs more contexts to help the audience assess its scientific standing. Most science and medical news is grounded on research findings; environmental reporting needs to do the same to gain credibility and give readers context (Logan, 2001: 24). Under such circumstances, what are the special qualities of a journalist needed to cover environmental issues? For this question, out of the total 162 respondents in the sample, 75.9 per cent reported that they give priority to understanding the issue (Table 31). However, 10.6 per cent thought getting the right information is important, 9.9 per cent said that identifying the right source is important. Two respondents each from the sample found that writing the report, on-the-spot study and contacting resource persons as the special qualities is needed.

Reliability of the Source

Journalists have a multitude of sources helping them to cover environmental issues. However, access to environmental information is limited and requires cross verification and expert's opinion to substantiate. How do the journalists in Kerala newspapers find information given by their sources reliable? Out of the total 162 respondents in the sample, 69.1 per cent thought that journalists rely on information given by sources while reporting on environmental issues. 19.8 per cent

Table–31
Special Qualities of a Journalist to Cover Environmental Issues as Reported by Respondents

Special Quality	*f*	%
Understanding of the issue	123	75.9
Getting the right information	17	10.6
Identifying the right sources	16	9.9
Writing the report	2	1.2
On-the-spot study	2	1.2
Contacting resource persons	2	1.2
Total	162	100

said that they can't say whether the sources are reliable or not and 11.1 per cent said that journalists don't rely on information given by sources.

Regarding respondent's perception of the best source to cover environmental issues, 49.4 per cent of the total 162 respondents found citizens as the best source in reporting environmental issues (Table 32). 27.8 per cent of the respondents thought research organizations as the best source and 18.5 per cent of the respondents find environmental agencies as the best source. Four (2.5%) respondents reported government departments as the best source. However two respondents said that self-investigation was important and one respondent said that he would contact resource persons based on the issue.

Among the respondents who preferred citizens as the best reliable source, 9.9 per cent belonged to *Malayala Manorama,* 9.3 per cent to *Deshabhimani,* 8.6 per cent to *Kerala Kaumudi,* 6.8 per cent *Mathrubhumi,* 6.2 per cent to *The Hindu* and 3.1 per cent to *Mangalam.* As much as 8.6 per cent of the respondents from *Malayala Manorama* viewed research organizations as the best reliable source whereas 3.7 per cent each of the respondents from *Mathrubhumi* and *The Hindu* cited environmental agencies as the best reliable source.

Table–32
Respondent's Perception of the Best Reliable Source to Cover Environmental Issues

Source	*f*	%
Citizens	80	49.4
Research organizations	45	27.8
Environmental agenciès	30	18.5
Government departments	4	2.5
Self-investigation	2	1.2
Resource persons on the issue	1	0.6
Total	162	100

Figure 4: Best Source to Cover Environmental Issues

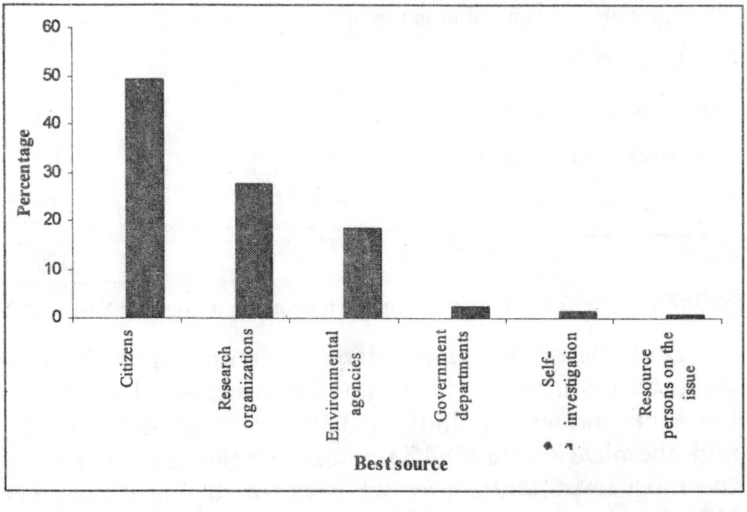

Regarding the verification of information given by a source, Table 33 shows that 39.9 per cent of the respondents reported that journalists do their cross-checking with experts in the subject area whereas 27.8 per cent of the respondents say journalists' cross-check with documents available on the issue. 7.3 per cent of the respondents say journalists' cross-check with the same source and 2.4 per cent of the respondents say that they do it through journalists from other newspapers. Four respondents said that journalists verify the information with NGOs working on the issue. One respondent said journalists' check with other sources and one respondent said they talk to affected people. However 19.7 per cent of the respondents reported that journalists use all the above sources to crosscheck the information in hand.

Table-33
Respondent's Perception of Verification of Information Given by a Source

Response	*% (n=208)*
By cross-checking with experts	39.9
Checking documents available on the issue	27.8
By cross-checking with the same source	7.3
Through journalists in other newspapers	2.4
Checking with other sources	0.5
Talking to affected people	0.5
By verifying with NGOs	1.9
All the above	19.7
Total	100

N=162 Since respondents gave multiple responses, it does not tally with N.

Table 34 shows respondent's perception of the most important source to cover some environmental issues. For issues like industrial pollution (43.8%), use of pesticides (45.1%) and chemical waste (58.1%), research agencies was cited as the most important source whereas for drying up of rivers (48.1%), destruction of paddy fields (54.9%), pollution of rivers/backwaters (41.9%), destruction of hills (46.9%) and sand mining (55.6%) citizens were cited as the most important source. For hazardous solid waste, 11.7 per cent of the respondents and for destruction of paddy fields 16.7 per cent of the respondents cited Government as the most important source. 24.7 per cent of the respondents cited NGOs as better

Table-34
Respondent's Perception of the most Important Source to Cover Some Environmental Issues

No.	*Environmental issue*	*Govt.* %	*Business* %	*Citizens* %	*NGOs* %	*Research Agencies* %	*Total* %
1.	Industrial pollution	4.9	2.5	29.6	19.2	43.8	100
2.	Drying up of rivers	3.7	-	48.1	19.1	29.1	100
3.	Hazardous solid waste	11.7	1.2	36.5	18.5	32.1	100
4.	Use of pesticides	8.6	1.9	28.3	16.1	45.1	100
5.	Chemical waste	8.6	1.9	14.2	17.2	58.1	100
6.	Destruction of paddy fields	16.7	-	54.9	15.5	12.9	100
7.	Pollution of rivers/back-waters	5.6	-	41.9	24.7	27.8	100
8.	Destruction of hills	14.8	-	46.9	24.7	13.6	100
9.	Deforestation	19.1	-	32.2	27.8	20.9	100
10.	Sand mining	8.6	1.2	55.6	17.3	17.3	100

source for covering issues on pollution of rivers/backwaters and an equal 24.7 per cent of the respondents marked NGOS as the important source to cover issues of destruction of hills whereas 27.8 per cent of the respondents said that NGOs are the best source to cover issues on deforestation. As low as 2.5 per cent of the respondents reported that business organizations were the best source to cover issues of industrial pollution.

Ethics

Ethics are guidelines that help in the smooth conduct of a profession. In the case of journalism, they monitor the process of dissemination of information (Murthy, 2004: 70). In environmental reporting, ethics mainly relate to favouring one party or the other involved in the issue through suppression of news one way or the other. Asked whether journalists favour parties involved in the issue while reporting, out of the total 162 respondents in the sample, 37.7 per cent of the respondents said that journalists do favour one party or the other while reporting on environmental issues (Table 35). However, 31.5 per cent of the respondents said that they don't favour and a close 30 per cent said that they couldn't say about it.

Table–35
Do Journalists Favour Parties Involved?

Response	*% (n=162)*
Yes	37.7
No	31.5
Can't say	30.8
Total	100

Out of the total 162 respondents in the sample, 30.2 per cent of the respondents said that journalists suppress news while reporting on environmental issues (Table 36). However, 37.1 per cent of the respondents said that they don't suppress news and 32.7 per cent said that they couldn't say about it.

Table–36
Do Journalists Suppress News While Reporting on Environment?

Response	*% (n=162)*
Yes	30.2
No	37.1
Can't say	32.7
Total	100

Out of the 61 respondents who said that journalists do suppress news while reporting on environment, more than half (55.7%) of the respondents said that they do it by supporting a particular side. 21.3 per cent of the respondents said that journalists do it by adding a personal outlook to the news item while writing it (Table 37). 8.2 per cent of the respondents opined that they do it by quoting non-existing sources and another 8.2 per cent said that journalists do it by manipulating their language. Two respondents each cited the methods of either hiding sensitive information or skipping issues of relevance.

Table–37
Respondent's Perception of News Suppression by Journalists

Perception	*f*	%
By quoting non-existing sources	5	8.2
By manipulating the language	5	8.2
By supporting a particular side	34	55.7
By including a personal outlook	13	21.3
Hiding sensitive information	2	3.3
Skipping issues of relevance	2	3.3
Total	61	100

Table 38 shows the perception of 61 respondents about journalists showing favours in news reports on environment. 36.1 per cent of the respondents said that journalists favour business organizations whereas 34.4 per cent reported that the journalists favour victims involved in the issue. Six respondents (9.9%) thought that journalists favour the government whereas one respondent thought journalists favour parties with vested interests in the issue and one respondent felt that journalists follow the policy of the newspaper while showing favours in news reports on environment.

Table–38
Respondent's Perception of Journalists Showing Favours in News Reports on Environment

Response	*f*	%
Business organizations	22	36.1
Victims involved in the issue	21	34.4
Environmentalists	10	16.4
Government	6	9.9
Vested interests	1	1.6
Depends on the policy of the newspaper	1	1.6
Total	61	100

6

Newspaper Coverage of Environmental Issues in Kerala

The present chapter presents results of newspaper coverage of environmental issues in two parts. Part I deals with the respondent's perception of newspaper coverage of environmental issues and their support to environmental issues. Part II gives details of content analysis of environmental issues of select newspapers.

PART–I
PERCEPTIONS OF PRINT JOURNALISTS

Mass media perform the role of informing the public about issues that affect their lives in addition to educating and entertaining them. The news media has a significant influence on society as a primary information source. This was validated in a survey of adults conducted by the American Opinion Research, Inc., (1993) when 81 per cent considered news media is their primary source of information on science topics, especially environmental and natural resources. Newspapers generally reflect the society's needs. However newspapers shift their focus with the changing preferences of readers to suit their tastes. Environment is a social issue and needs the attention of newspapers for sustainability. Are newspapers in Kerala giving enough coverage to environmental issues? Are they able to influence the authorities in solving them? How can the management of the newspaper support the journalists in reporting on environmental beat? What are the perceptions of coverage of major environmental issues in Kerala? An attempt was made to ascertain the perception of the respondents on the newspaper coverage of environmental issues in Kerala.

News Items

What do journalists think about newspaper readers' preference in news items? For this question, 53.2 per cent respondents reported that readers seek political news stories in newspapers followed by (30.9%) who reported that readers seek human-interest stories and (12.9%) who reported entertainment stories (Table 39). Environment stories had the lowest percentage of 0.6 per cent. No respondent felt that newspaper readers in Kerala seek sensational and crime stories.

Table-39
Respondent's Perception of Readers' Preference in News Items

S. No.	*News Item*	*f*	*% (n=162)*
1.	Political	86	53.2
2.	Human interest	50	30.9
3.	Entertainment	21	12.9
4.	Sports	2	1.2
5.	Environment	1	0.6
6.	Health and education	2	1.2
7.	Sensational/crime	0	0
	Total		100

Influence

As newspapers influence public opinion on issues, they are expected to play a constructive role in contributing to positive trends in the society. Coverage of environmental issues in newspapers is supposed to create environmental awareness among people so as to result in citizen action. It is also supposed to influence the authorities and agencies to take steps in solving them. Therefore an attempt was made in the study to ascertain that the environmental news would influence which section in the society. Out of the 162 respondents, a majority of respondents (90.1%) said that society learns much about environment through newspapers. However, 2.5 per cent reported that they couldn't say about it. And out of the total respondents who felt that society learns much about environment through newspapers, 98.6 per cent said that environmental reports in the newspapers do influence the society. A minority of 0.7 per cent opined that they don't influence the society and another 0.7 per cent said can't say about it.

Table-40
Who is Influenced Most by News Reports on Environment?

Response	*% (n=144)*
Readers	87.5
Government	7.6
Politicians	2.1
NGOs	2.8
Total	100

N=162

Asked about who is influenced most, a majority of 87.5 per cent respondents said that readers would be influenced through environmental news reports (Table 40). 7.6 per cent said that Government would be influenced most. 2.8 per cent of the respondents opined that NGOs could be influenced closely followed by 2.1 per cent respondents who said that politicians would be influenced.

Quality of Reporting

Environmental issues receive the much needed attention from the people as well as from the Government machinery, when they are covered by newspapers adequately.

Table–41
Respondent's Opinion of the Quality of Environmental Reporting in Kerala Newspapers

Respondent's Opinion	*% (n=162)*
Very good	3.1
Good	54.3
Poor	38.3
Very poor	4.3
Total	100

Therefore, respondents were asked to measure quality of environmental reporting in Kerala newspapers on a four-point scale viz. very good, good, bad and very bad. Further, more than 54 per cent of the respondents rated that quality of environmental reporting was good although 38.3 per cent of the respondents said that environmental coverage was poor (Table 41). However, 4.3 per cent of the respondents reported that quality of environmental reporting was very poor and 3.1 per cent said that quality of reporting was very good.

Table–42
Newspaper-wise Respondent's View of Coverage of Environmental Issues in Kerala Newspapers

Opinion	*Newspaper*						
	Malayala Manorama (n=35) %	*Mathru-bhumi (n=25) %*	*Deshabhi-mani (n=23) %*	*Kerala Kaumudi (n=21). %*	*Mangalam (n=17) %*	*The New Indian Express (n=18) %*	*The Hindu (n=23) %*
Very good	-	4	-	4.8	-	5.5	8.7
Good	40	64	43.5	47.6	52.9	66.7	78.2
Poor	57.1	24	56.5	33.3	47.1	27.8	13.1
Very poor	2.9	8	-	14.3	-	-	-
Total	100	100	100	100	100	100	100

N=162

A majority of the respondents across the seven selected newspapers rated the coverage as good (Table 42). However 57.1 per cent of the respondents from *Malayala Manorama* said that the coverage was poor followed by 56.5 per cent from *Deshabhimani* and 47.1 per cent from *Mangalam.* 14.3 per cent respondents from *Kerala Kaumudi* opined that coverage was very poor and from *The Hindu* 8.7 per cent of the respondents said that the coverage was very good followed by 5.5 per cent from *The New Indian Express.*

Table 43 describes the respondents' perception of coverage given to certain major environmental issues by Kerala newspapers. The perception was rated at three levels: high, medium and low. For industrial pollution, nearly 50 per cent of the respondents rated medium and 28.4 per cent high. The issue of use of pesticides was rated as medium by 46.9 per cent and high by 33.3 per cent. The issue of chemical waste was rated as low by 50.7 per cent and medium by 40.7 per cent. Out of the 162 respondents, 46.3 per cent of the respondents rated destruction of paddy fields as medium. In the case of pollution of rivers and backwaters, 45.8 per cent of the respondents found the issue of medium importance followed by 33.9 per cent who found it to be of high importance.

Table-43
Respondents' Perception of Coverage of Major Environmental Issues in Kerala

S. No.	*Major Issues*	*High* %	*Medium* %	*Low* %	*Total*
1.	Industrial pollution	28.4 (46)	50 (81)	21.6 (35)	100
2.	Drying up of rivers	42.6 (69)	42 (68)	15.4 (25)	100
3.	Hazardous solid waste disposal	33.3 (54)	41.4 (67)	25.3 (41)	100
4.	Use of pesticides	33.3 (54)	46.9 (76)	19.8 (32)	100

Contd...

S. No.	Major Issues	High %	Medium %	Low %	Total
5.	Chemical waste	8.6 (14)	40.7 (66)	50.7 (82)	100
6.	Destruction of paddy fields	25.9 (42)	46.3 (75)	27.8 (45)	100
7.	Pollution of rivers/ backwaters	33.9 (55)	45.8 (74)	20.3 (33)	100
8.	Destruction of hills	9.9 (16)	41.4 (67)	48.7 (79)	100
9.	Deforestation	21.6 (35)	49.4 (80)	29 (47)	100
10.	Sand mining	48.2 (78)	36.4 (59)	15.4 (25)	100
Total					

Note: The figures in parenthesis are frequencies.

News Genre

News items should be presented to public without reducing the seriousness of the issue. It is the art of converting complicated news stories into compelling reads. Do news stories on environmental issues require special style of writing to create a better impact without diluting the importance of the issue? Table 44 shows news genre preferred by respondents in writing environmental issues. 45.7 per cent of the respondents preferred to write the story as news item followed by 42.6 per cent who preferred to write as feature stories. 7.4 per cent said that they would prefer to choose the genre depending on the issue. Nevertheless 4.3 per cent opted for human-interest angle for environment new items.

Training

Does environmental reporting require special training for the journalists to cover environmental topics accurately with proper context and scientific grounding? Environmental

Table–44
News Genre Preferred by Respondents in Writing Environmental Issues

News Genre	*f*	%
Feature	69	42.6
News item	74	45.7
Human interest story	7	4.3
Depends on the issue	12	7.4
Total	162	100

reporting is like science reporting and includes technical matter to be reported. Training can also provide journalist better understanding in choosing topics, sources and story angles. Asked whether training is needed for journalists to cover environmental issues better, a majority of 96.2 per cent said that better training is required for journalists in covering environmental issues.

Table–45
Type of Training Required for Journalists in Covering Environmental Issues

Response	*f*	% *(n=172)*
Periodic training	40	23.2
Special courses on environment	90	52.4
Exposure to expert's lectures	40	23.2
Self-study	2	1.2
Total		100

N=162. Since respondents gave multiple responses, it does not tally with N.

Regarding the type of training 52.4 per cent preferred to have special courses on environment (Table 45). 23.2 per cent each preferred periodic training and expert's lectures. However 1.2 per cent said that self-study could lead to better understanding of the issue.

Role of Newspaper Management

Newspaper management has a key role in determining the quality of coverage of environmental issues. It plays a key role in determining the allocation of journalistic time, resources and space for coverage of environment news. To the question can newspaper management play a key role in promoting coverage of environment, 83.3 per cent thought that it could play a key role. About 7 per cent said that management could not play any role and 9.9 per cent said that they couldn't say about it.

Table 46 explains respondents' opinion on how newspaper management can support coverage of environmental issues. 29.6 per cent of the respondents said that management should give more space for environmental news. 20.8 per cent said that it could be through better environment friendly editorial policies. 14.8 per cent of the respondents reported that better training should be given to the journalists by the management to report on environmental issues. Another 14.8 per cent suggested setting up a team of environmental journalists in each newspaper bureau whereas 12.6 per cent of the respondents needed moral support and 7.4 per cent needed more freedom in the coverage.

Table–46
Respondent's Opinion of How Newspaper Management can Support Coverage of Environmental Issues

Respondent's Opinion	*% (n=135)*
Give more space for environmental issues	29.6
Have environment friendly editorial policy	20.8
Provide better training for journalists	14.8
Appoint team of environmental journalists in each bureau	14.8
Give moral support	12.6
Give more freedom in coverage	7.4
Total	100

Because newspapers are a source of information for the general public, they play a significant role in creating awareness among people on environmental issues. However, environment beat might be expected to be particularly difficult to describe because it represents an area of rapid change (Witt, 1974). Hence in this context, an attempt was made to ascertain the perceptions of respondents related to the coverage of environmental issues.

Legal Knowledge

Environmental reporting involves considerable amount of risk for the journalists including legal problems. Out of the total 162 respondents, 74.7 per cent of the respondents have reported that journalists do face legal problems when they report environmental conflict. However, 13.6 per cent of the respondents have viewed that journalists will not face legal problems. The remaining 11.7 per cent respondents have not expressed either of the views.

However, majority (88.3%) of the respondents have opined that journalists do need special legal knowledge necessary while reporting on environmental issues, whereas 7.4 per cent of the respondents said that it was not necessary to have legal knowledge and 4.3 per cent said that they were not sure about it.

Risk

Other than legal problems, journalists on environmental beat face other kinds of risk as well. At times there can be physical violence, harassment or even a clash with the management. Out of the total 162 respondents, 81.4 per cent of the respondents have reported that journalists do face risks when they report on environment. However, 9.3 per cent of the respondents have viewed that they don't face any kind of risk, yet 9.3 per cent feel that they can't say about it.

As regards the kind of risk faced by journalists while reporting environmental issues, 34.6 per cent of the respondents reported that they face legal problems whereas

Table–47
Type of Risk Involved in Reporting Environmental Issues

Type of Risk	*% (n=199)*
Legal problems	34.6
Physical violence	31.2
Harassment	30.7
Loss of employment	3.5
Total	100

N= 162. Since respondents gave multiple responses, it does not tally with N.

31.2 per cent of the respondents said that they face physical violence and 30.7 per cent of the respondents said that they faced harassment and 3.5 per cent of the respondents said that they feared loss of employment (Table 47).

Journalist's Support to the Environment

As journalists report on issues from the field, they need to have a special interest in the subject for a better understanding. Can journalists support environmental issues in a better way? Questions were asked to ascertain journalists' perception on the issue. Table 48 shows respondent's opinion on how journalists in Kerala can support environment. 42.5 per cent of the respondents are of the opinion that they can support environment by creating awareness among readers through wider coverage whereas 28.5 per cent of the respondents felt that journalists should undertake investigative studies on environmental issues, and 22.2 per cent feel that they should report more environmental stories and try to give prominence. 5.6 per cent respondents felt that journalists should take up special themes on environment on a regular basis.

Major Environmental Issues

How do journalists in Kerala newspapers rank the various major environmental issues in Kerala? Table 49 shows respondent's perception of major environmental issues in Kerala.

Table–48
Respondent's Opinion on How Journalists in Kerala can Support Environment

Respondent's Opinion	*% (n=193)*
Creating awareness among readers through wider coverage	42.5
Making investigative studies on issues	28.5
Giving prominence to environmental stories	22.2
Undertaking special themes on a regular basis	5.6
Forcing Government to make effective legislations	0.6
Taking up local issues	0.6
Total	100

N=162. Since respondents gave multiple responses, it does not tally with N.

Out of the 162 respondents, about 21 per cent considered drying up of rivers as a major environmental issue at present followed by 16.1 per cent reported destruction of paddy fields as the major issue. 15.4 per cent and 14.8 per cent respondents respectively reported pollution of rivers/backwaters and hazardous solid waste disposal as major environmental issues. They were followed by deforestation (9.3%), sand mining (7.4%), use of pesticides (6.8%), industrial pollution (6.8%), and destruction of hills (2.5%).

Table–49
Respondent's Perception of Major Environmental Issues in Kerala

S. No.	*Major Issue*	*f*	*%*
1.	Drying up of rivers	34	20.9
2.	Destruction of paddy fields	26	16.1
3.	Pollution of rivers/backwaters	25	15.4
4.	Hazardous solid waste disposal	24	14.8

Contd...

S. No.	Major Issue	f	%
5.	Deforestation	15	9.3
6.	Sand mining	12	7.4
7.	Use of pesticides	11	6.8
8.	Industrial pollution	11	6.8
9.	Destruction of hills	4	2.5
	Total	162	100

Specific Environmental Issue

Majority of the respondents from the selected newspapers in four cities reported endosulphan pesticide issue in Kasargode district, Plachimada Coca Cola issue, sand mining, forest encroachment issue, drinking water problem, destruction of paddy fields etc., as major specific environmental issues projected well during the last 5 years by the Kerala newspapers.

Table 50 shows that 31.4 per cent respondents reported the issue of spraying of endosulphan pesticide on the cashew crops in Kasargode district, while 23.4 per cent of the respondents reported the Coca Cola plant issue of exploiting ground water resources in Palghat district. 13.6 per cent of the respondents viewed sand mining as the most important issue. The issue of Government's resistance to the encroachment by tribal people into the forestland at Mathikettan area in Thiruvananthapuram district was reported by 6.2 per cent. However, 3.1 per cent each reported industrial pollution, deforestation and destruction of paddy fields as the one specific environmental issue projected well in the newspapers during the last five years and 1.2 per cent of the respondents found waste disposal as a well-projected issue.

Table 51 gives the city-wise distribution of respondent's view of one specific environment issue that was projected well by newspapers in Kerala in the last five years. Nearly 40 per cent of the respondents found endosulphan pesticide issue as

Table-50
Respondent's View of one Specific Environmental Issue Projected well in the Newspapers During the Last 5 Years

Specific Environmental Issue	*f*	%
Endosulphan pesticide issue	51	31.4
Plachimada Coca Cola issue	38	23.4
Sand mining	22	13.6
Forest encroachment issue	10	6.2
Drinking water problem	9	5.6
Pollution of Periyar river	6	3.7
Pollution of rivers and backwaters	3	1.9
Industrial pollution	5	3.1
Deforestation	5	3.1
Destruction of paddy fields	5	3.1
Drying up of rivers	3	1.9
Hydel projects	1	0.6
Pesticide in soft drinks	1	0.6
Waste disposal	2	1.2
Clay mining	1	0.6
Total	162	100

the best covered issue whereas in Kottayam district 25.6 per cent of the respondents reported Coca Cola issue as the well projected issue. 21.4 per cent and 46.8 per cent of the respondents respectively from Kottayam and Kozhikode cited endosulphan issue as the well-projected issue.

Thiruvananthapuram is the capital of Kerala and the headquarters of Thiruvananthapuram district. The city is the largest and most populous city in Kerala with an urban agglomeration having a population of about 7,45,000. The city has major environmental problems like pollution of rivers,

Table-51
City-wise Distribution of Respondent's Perception of one Specific Environmental Issue Projected Well During the Last Five Years

	City			
Specific Environmental Issue in Newspapers	*Thiruvananthapuram (n=49)*	*Kottayam (n=39)*	*Kochi (n=42)*	*Kozhikode (n=32)*
Endosulphan pesticide issue	36.6	23.1	21.4	46.8
Plachimada Coca Cola issue	28.5	25.6	19	18.8
Sand mining	14.2	7.7	14.2	18.8
Forest encroachment issue	4.1	15.4	4.8	–
Drinking water problem	4.1	5.1	4.8	9.4
Pollution of Periyar river	–	–	16.6	–
Pollution of rivers and backwaters	2.1	2.6	2.4	–
Industrial pollution	2.1	–	4.8	3.1
Deforestation	4.1	7.7	–	–
Destruction of paddy fields	2.1	5.1	2.4	3.1
Drying up of rivers	–	5.1	2.4	–
Hydel projects	–	–	2.4	–
Pesticide in soft drinks	–	–	2.4	–
Waste disposal	–	2.6	2.4	–
Clay mining	2.1	–	–	–
Total	100	100	100	100

N=162

problems of drinking water and sand mining. A number of large, medium and small industries in the industrial area cause adverse effects on health of the people. The heavy pollution of the downstream stretches of Karamana River and the Killi River by raw sewage discharged from city drains and the heavily polluted Parvathy Puthanar canal create major health hazards. Heavy dust precipitation in certain areas because of the atmospheric pollution by factories causes respiratory diseases and allergic reactions among the people.

In Thiruvananthapuram, a majority (71.4%) of the respondents from *Deshabhimani*, 50 per cent from *The New Indian Express*, 42.9 per cent from *Mathrubhumi* and 40 per cent from *The Hindu* perceived that endosulphan pesticide issue was reported well (Table 52) whereas 50 per cent of the respondents from *Mangalam*, nearly 46 per cent from *Kerala Kaumudi* and 43 per cent from *Mathrubhumi* opined that Plachimada Coca Cola issue was projected well during the last five years. A majority of 33.3 per cent from *Malayala Manorama* viewed Plachimada Coca Cola issue and sand mining as well projected whereas 30 per cent from *The Hindu* perceived that sand mining was well projected. 25 per cent each from *Mangalam* reported destruction of paddy fields and clay mining as major issues projected well.

Table–52
Thiruvananthapuram: Respondent's Perception of One Specific Environmental Issue Projected Well During the Last Five Years

Specific Environmental Issue in Newspapers	*Newspaper*						
	Malayala Manorama (n=6)	*Mathrubhumi (n=7)*	*Deshabhimani (n=7)*	*Kerala Kaumudi (n=11)*	*Mangalam (n=4)*	*The New Indian Express (n=4)*	*The Hindu (n=10)*
Endosulphan pesticide issue	16.7	42.9	71.4	27.3	-	50	40
Plachimada Coca Cola issue	33.3	42.9	14.3	45.5	50	25	-

Contd...

Specific Environmental Issue in Newspapers	*Newspaper*						
	Malayala Manorama (n=6)	*Mathrubhumi (n=7)*	*Deshabhimani (n=7)*	*Kerala Kaumudi (n=11)*	*Mangalam (n=4)*	*The New Indian Express (n=4)*	*The Hindu (n=10)*
Sand mining	33.3	–	–	18.1	–	–	30
Forest encroachment issue	16.7	–	–	–	–	–	10
Drinking water problem	–	14.2	–	–	–	–	10
Pollution of Periyar river	–	–	–	–	–	–	–
Pollution of rivers and backwaters	–	–	14.3	–	–	–	–
Industrial pollution	–	–	–	–	–	25	–
Deforestation	–	–	–	9.1	–	–	10
Destruction of paddy fields	–	–	–	–	25	–	–
Drying up of rivers	–	–	–	–	–	–	–
Hydel projects	–	–	–	–	–	–	–
Pesticide in soft drinks	–	–	–	–	–	–	–
Waste disposal	–	–	–	–	–	–	–
Clay mining	–	–	–	–	25	–	–
Total	100	100	100	100	100	100	100

N=49

Kottayam is a city and a municipality and is a major trading centre of commercial crops and a publishing centre in Kerala. It is the administrative capital of Kottayam district. In 1989 it achieved the distinction of being the first municipal town in India to achieve 100 per cent literacy. As per the 2001 census, Kottayam municipality had a population of 60,725. Extensive cultivation of rubber trees has made Kottayam a major trading place of natural rubber in India. The city has major environmental problems related to siltation, growth of weeds, deteriorating water quality, growth of pests and rodents and spread of vector borne seasonal diseases. The city also suffers due to improper waste management and wastewater management. The Meenachil river, the main source of drinking water for the city is contaminated due to the emptying of wastewater from the hotels, hospitals, drains and medical laboratories into the river. The wastewater from hotels and toilets in nearby towns also gets diverted into the river.

In Kottayam 80 per cent of the respondents from *Deshabhimani* rated endosulphan pesticide issue as the well-projected issue whereas 60 per cent of respondents from *Kerala Kaumudi* found Plachimada Coca Cola issue projected well. While 25 per cent from *Malayala Manorama* rated endosulphan pesticide issue and 18.7 per cent rated Plachimada Coca Cola issue, 12.5 per cent each supported issues related to drinking water, deforestation and drying up of rivers as well projected. While 33 per cent from *Mathrubhumi* supported Plachimada Coca Cola issue, 16.7 per cent each viewed issues like endosulphan pesticide, forest encroachment issue, waste disposal and deforestation as well projected issues (Table 53).

Kochi or Cochin is one of the principal seaports of the country and is located in the Ernakulam district of Kerala. The city has an estimated population of 650,000, with an extended metropolitan population of over 1.6 million, making it the second largest city in the state with a large urban agglomeration. Vast urbanization and inadequate sewage treatment have led to pollution of network of backwaters in and around the city. Inadequate waste disposal system creates

Table–53
Kottayam: Respondent's Perception of one Specific Environmental Issue Projected Well During the Last Five Years

Specific Environmental Issue in Newspapers	*Newspaper*						
	Malayala Manorama (n=16)	*Mathrubhumi (n=6)*	*Deshabhimani (n=5)*	*Kerala Kaumudi (n=5)*	*Mangalam (n=5)*	*The New Indian Express (n=1)*	*The Hindu (n=1)*
Endosulphan pesticide issue	25	16.7	80	–	–	–	–
Plachimada Coca Cola issue	18.7	33.2	–	60	40	–	–
Sand mining	6.3	–	–	20	20	–	–
Forest encroachment issue	6.3	16.7	20	–	20	–	–
Drinking water problem	12.5	–	–	–	–	100	100
Pollution of Periyar river	–	–	–	–	–	–	–
Pollution of rivers and backwaters	–	–	–	–	20	–	–
Industrial pollution	–	–	–	–	–	–	–
Deforestation	12.5	16.7	–	–	–	–	–
Destruction of paddy fields	6.2	–	–	20	–	–	–
Drying up of rivers	12.5	–	–	–	–	–	–

Contd...

Specific Environmental Issue in Newspapers	*Newspaper*						
	Malayala Manorama (n=16)	*Mathrubhumi (n=6)*	*Deshabhimani (n=5)*	*Kerala Kaumudi (n=5)*	*Mangalam (n=5)*	*The New Indian Express (n=1)*	*The Hindu (n=1)*
Hydel projects	-	-	-	-	-	-	-
Pesticide in soft drinks	-	-	-	-	-	-	-
Waste disposal	-	16.7	-	-	-	-	-
Clay mining	-	-	-	-	-	-	-
Total	100	100	100	100	100	100	100

N=39

flooding in rainfall season thereby contaminating soil and water resources. Vehicular pollution and urban waste are other major problems. The Periyar river carries large quantity of domestic, industrial and agricultural pollutants to the urban area from the nearby factories. Large scale land reclamation and sand quarrying in the city limits have resulted in the removal of topsoil and has deteriorated the soil quality.

In Kochi, 50 per cent of the respondents from *Mathrubhumi*, 66.7 per cent from *Mangalam* and 33 per cent of respondents from *Deshabhimani* and *Kerala Kaumudi* thought that endosulphan pesticide issue was projected well during the last five years. However, 37.5 per cent of respondents from *Malaya Manorama* and 33.3 per cent respondents each from *Kerala Kaumudi* and *Mangalam* thought Plachimada Coca Cola issue was projected well (Table 54). 33.3 per cent of the respondents from *The New Indian Express* thought that sand mining issue was well projected whereas 33.3 per cent from *Kerala Kaumudi* supported pollution of Periyar river as the well projected issue by Kerala newspapers. 16.7 per cent of the respondents from *Deshabhimani* reported destruction of paddy fields and 12.5 per cent of respondents from *Malayala Manorama* opined that waste disposal were the environmental issues that were covered well.

Table-54

Kochi: Respondent's Perception of One Specific Environmental Issue Projected Well During the Last Five Years

Specific Environ-mental Issue in Newspapers	*Newspaper*						
	Malayala Manorama (n=8)	*Mathru-bhumi (n=4)*	*Deshabhi-mani (n=6)*	*Kerala Kaumudi (n=3)*	*Mangalam (n=3)*	*The New Indian Express (n=9)*	*The Hindu (n=9)*
Endosulphan pesticide issue	12.5	50	33.2	33.3	66.7	-	11.1
Plachimada Coca Cola issue	37.5	-	-	33.3	33.3	11.1	22.2
Sand mining	12.5	-	-	-	-	33.3	22.2
Forest en-croachment issue	-	-	16.7	-	-	11.1	-
Drinking water problem	12.5	25	-	-	-	-	-
Pollution of Periyar river	12.5	25	-	33.3	-	33.3	11.1
Pollution of rivers and backwaters	-	-	16.7	-	-	-	-
Industrial pollution	-	-	16.7	-	-	11.2	-
Deforestation	-	-	-	-	-	-	-
Destruction of paddy fields	-	-	16.7	-	-	-	-

Contd...

Specific Environmental Issue in Newspapers	*Newspaper*						
	Malayala Manorama (n=8)	*Mathrubhumi (n=4)*	*Deshabhimani (n=6)*	*Kerala Kaumudi (n=3)*	*Mangalam (n=3)*	*The New Indian Express (n=9)*	*The Hindu (n=9)*
Drying up of rivers	-	-	-	-	-	-	11.1
Hydel projects	-	-	-	-	-	-	11.1
Pesticide in soft drinks	-	-	-	-	-	-	11.1
Waste disposal	12.5	-	-	-	-	-	-
Clay mining	-	-	-	-	-	-	-
Total	100	100	100	100	100	100	100

N=42

Kozhikode or Calicut is the third largest city in Kerala and has a population of 801,190 and is the headquarters of Kozhikode district. It is the nodal point for all districts in the northern region and has been traditionally developed as a centre for forest and agro-based industries. Kozhikode city was declared India's first litter-free city in 2004. However, the city continues to have its share of environmental problems. Bacteriological and chemical contamination of well water has made drinking water. Decreasing groundwater recharge due to changes in land use, destruction of mangroves due to encroachment, toxic and biomedical waste are the emerging problems. The closure of the polluting unit of Grasim Industries at Mavoor on the northern bank of river Chaliyar was a major environmental campaign that led to the closure of the industry.

All respondents from *Kerala Kaumudi* in Kozhikode reported that endosulphan pesticide issue was well projected in the last five years followed by 80 per cent from *Deshabhimani,* 60 per cent from *Mangalam* and 50 per cent from *Mathrubhumi,* whereas all respondents from *The New Indian Express* thought sand mining was the major issue projected well (Table 55). 40 per cent of respondents each from *Malayala Manorama* supported Plachimada Coca Cola issue and drinking water problem issue whereas 33.3 per cent of respondents from *The Hindu* cited drinking water problem issue as the major issue projected well.

Table–55
Kozhikode: Respondent's Perception of one Specific Environmental Issue Projected Well During the Last Five Years

Specific Environmental Issue in Newspapers	*Newspaper*						
	Malayala Manorama (n=5)	*Mathrubhumi (n=8)*	*Deshabhimani (n=5)*	*Kerala Kaumudi (n=2)*	*Mangalam (n=5)*	*The New Indian Express (n=4)*	*The Hindu (n=5)*
Endosulphan pesticide issue	-	50	80	100	60	-	66.7
Plachimada Coca Cola issue	40	25	20	-	20	-	-
Sand mining	20	12.5	-	-	-	100	-
Forest encroachment issue	-	-	-	-	-	-	-
Drinking water problem	40	-	-	-	-	-	33.3
Pollution of Periyar river	-	-	-	-	-	-	-
Pollution of rivers and backwaters	-	-	-	-	-	-	-
Industrial pollution	-	-	-	-	20	-	-

Contd...

Specific Environmental Issue in Newspapers	Newspaper						
	Malayala Manorama (n=5)	Mathrubhumi (n=8)	Deshabhimani (n=5)	Kerala Kaumudi (n=2)	Mangalam (n=5)	The New Indian Express (n=4)	The Hindu (n=5)
Deforestation	-	-	-	-	-	-	-
Destruction of paddy fields	-	12.5	-	-	-	-	-
Drying up of rivers	-	-	-	-	-	-	-
Hydel projects	-	-	-	-	-	-	-
Pesticide in soft drinks	-	-	-	-	-	-	-
Waste disposal	-	-	-	-	-	-	-
Clay mining	-	-	-	-	-	-	-
Total	100	100	100	100	100	100	100

N=32

Commitment

Commitment from the journalist is an important criterion that determines the quality of reporting. Commitment can also make the journalist socially responsible and work towards making an environmental issue receive better attention. They can make in-depth study of the issue, convince the management and report the issue in the right perspective.

Out of the 162 respondents, 85.2 per cent of the respondents reported that journalist's commitment to environment could improve reporting. 4.3 per cent of the respondents said no and 10.5 per cent said that they couldn't say about it (Table 56).

Table–56
Can Journalist's Commitment to Environment Improve Reporting?

Response	*No.*	*%*
Yes	138	85.2
No	7	4.3
Cannot say	17	10.5
Total	N=162	100

Table–57
Type of Commitment Described by Respondent to Improve Environmental Reporting

Type of Commitment	*% (n=138)*
Through better involvement with the issues	16.7
Studying issues better	22.5
Filing stories in the right perspective	15.2
Consider environment a social responsibility	17.4
Convincing management to take up issues	5.1
Undertaking investigative studies	21.7
Yes, but cannot describe	1.4
Total	100

Out of the 138 respondents who said that journalist's commitment to environment can improve reporting, 22.5 per cent of the respondents said that journalists should study the issue better (Table 57). This is closely followed by 21.7 per cent of the respondents who said that better commitment could develop interest to undertake and publish investigative studies. 17.4 per cent of the respondents thought that environment is a social responsibility and needs commitment on the part of the journalists whereas 16.7 per cent of the respondents thought that commitment could lead to better involvement with the issues. However, 15.2 per cent of the respondents felt that filing stories in the right perspective could show his or her commitment while 5.1 per cent of the respondents said that they could convince the management in reporting an issue.

Role of Newspapers in Environmental Issues

How can newspapers create environmental awareness among people? Out of the 162 respondents, a majority of 92.6 per cent respondents thought that newspapers could campaign on various environmental issues simultaneously. In this context, 83.3 per cent reported that there is an increased awareness on environmental issues among the people through coverage of newspapers in Kerala. However 10.4 per cent of the respondents felt that newspapers have not increased awareness and 12.3 per cent of the respondents said that they couldn't say about it.

Table–58
Ways to Project Important Environmental Issues

Response	*% (n=187)*
Having special issues and columns on environment	31.1
Publishing environment reports on front page with prominent headlines	20.3
Through setting up of special environment team of journalists	20.8
Undertaking special campaigns to initiate public dialogue	27.8
Total	100

N=162. Since respondents gave multiple responses, it did not tally with N.

Coming to newspapers' role in projecting environment as an important issue, 31.1 per cent of the respondents reported that there is a need to have special issues and columns on environment (Table 58). About 28 per cent of the respondents said that newspapers should undertake special campaigns to initiate public dialogue. Setting up of special environment team of journalists (20.8%) and publishing environment reports on front page with prominent headlines (20.3%) were the other responses.

In relation to the treatment given by newspapers to improve readership, out of the 162 respondents, 68.5 per cent of the respondents reported that environmental stories could be published on the first page (Table 59). About 18 per cent of the respondents however said that attractive headlines could help in improving readership. 8.7 per cent of the respondents preferred "box items" and 4.9 per cent suggested publishing of special pullouts on environment. All the 162 respondents agreed that photographs would increase readership of environmental issues in a newspaper.

Table-59
What Kind of Treatment can be Given to Environmental Stories to Improve Readership?

Response	*f*	%
By publishing them on the front page	111	68.5
By giving attractive headlines	29	17.9
As box items	14	8.7
By publishing special pullouts	8	4.9
Total	162	100

Out of the 162 respondents, 63 per cent of the respondents said that newspaper is effective in creating awareness on environment while 32.2 per cent of the respondents said that television is effective. About 5 per cent preferred other media like radio, books, Internet and traditional media to be effective in creating awareness on environment (Table 60).

Incentives

Can better incentives for journalists improve environmental reporting? To this specific question, 44 per cent of the respondents thought that special incentives from the Government could encourage environmental reporting. However

Table-60
Which Media do you Think is Effective in Creating Awareness on Environment?

Response	*f*	%
Newspaper	102	63.0
Television	52	32.2
Radio	2	1.2
Books	2	1.2
Internet	2	1.2
Traditional media	2	1.2
Total	162	100

41.4 per cent reported that special incentives would not make any difference and 14.2 per cent of the respondents could not say anything to this question.

Table-61
Type of Best Incentive Described by Respondents to Encourage Environmental Reporting

Incentive	*f*	*%(n=72)*
Special cash awards	26	36.1
Free transport facilities	17	23.6
Free training on environment	29	40.3
Total	72	100

Out of the 72 respondents who described that special incentives from the Government could encourage environmental reporting, 40.3 per cent preferred free training on environmental reporting (Table 61). 36.1 per cent viewed special cash awards as the best incentive and 23.6 per cent reported that free transport facilities could encourage environmental reporting.

Literacy and Environmental Awareness

Kerala was the first state in India which attained 100 per cent literacy. Has better literacy rate increased environmental awareness through newspapers? Out of the 162 respondents in the sample, 70.9 per cent said that literacy programmes in Kerala had an impact on awareness on environment followed by 18.6 per cent who said that there had been no impact. 10.5 per cent of the respondents said that they can't say anything to the question.

Role of Media in Environmental Education

Environmental education is an important tool in increasing environmental awareness among the people. There are various agencies like non-governmental organizations and nature clubs working towards this goal. Should newspapers join hands with such agencies in educating people on environment? Can newspapers support initiatives by Government or NGOs on environmental education? For this question, out of the 162 respondents in the sample, majority of 90.1 per cent reported that newspapers could support initiatives on environmental education. However, 3.7 per cent said that newspapers could not support such initiatives and 6.2 per cent answered can't say.

Table–62
How can Newspapers Support Initiatives for Environmental Education?

Response	*No.*	*%*
Giving better coverage on such initiatives	78	45.1
Encouraging schools to take up nature campaigns	65	37.6
Awareness through mass media partnerships	23	13.2
Supporting folk media in spreading awareness	7	4.1
Total	173	100

N=162. Since respondents gave multiple responses, the total does not tally with N.

Table 62 explains about the perceptions of the respondents to support initiatives on environmental education especially at grassroots levels, schools etc. 45.1 per cent of the respondents reported that newspapers should give better coverage on such initiatives in their newspapers. 37.6 per cent of the respondents said that newspapers could encourage schools to undertake nature campaigns whereas 13.2 per cent of the respondents felt that newspapers should work in tandem with other mass media for better initiatives and 4.1 per cent said that newspapers and folk media could join hands together for the purpose.

Table-63
Can Journalists Influence the Management to take up Environmental Campaigns?

Response	*f*	%
Yes	91	56.2
No	36	22.2
Cannot say	35	21.6
Total	162	100

Table 63 shows the respondents' opinion on journalists influencing the management to take up environmental campaigns. 56.2 per cent of the respondents felt that journalists could influence the management in taking up environmental campaigns while 22.2 per cent reported negatively. Whereas 83.3 per cent of the respondents reported that management could play a key role in improving environmental reporting.

PART-II
CONTENT ANALYSIS OF SELECT NEWSPAPERS

In order to ascertain coverage given to environmental issues *vis-à-vis* other news items, content analysis technique was used. A total of 350 newspaper editions of seven dailies covering four cities viz., Thiruvananthapuram, Kottayam, Kochi and Kozhikode have been analyzed for the purpose. In the analysis, it was found that *Mangalam* (3.7%) followed by *Deshabhimani* (3%) allocated more percentage of news items to environment as compared to other newspapers in terms of frequency of news items. However, all the newspapers did not allocate more than four per cent of news items to environment (Table 64).

Table–64
Total Number of News Items Analyzed: Newspaper-wise

Newspaper	*News Items*				*Total*
	Environment		*Others*		
	No.	*%*	*No.*	*%*	
Malayala Manorama	48	2.7	1750	97.3	100
Mathrubhumi	42	2.6	1568	97.4	100
Deshabhimani	48	3.0	1568	97.0	100
Kerala Kaumudi	22	1.7	1302	98.3	100
Mangalam	46	3.7	1176	96.3	100
The New Indian Express	30	2.7	1064	97.3	100
The Hindu	46	2.9	1596	97.1	100

N=14

Figure 5: Coverage Given to Environment by Select Newspapers

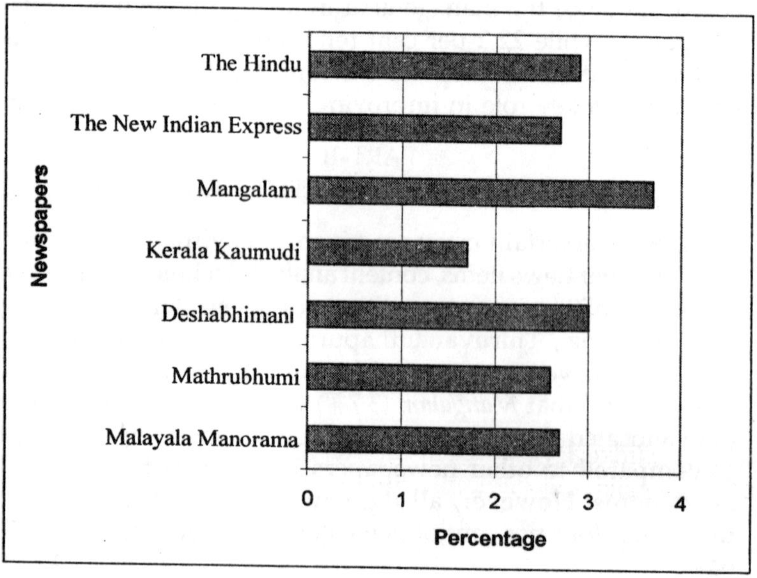

However, in the analysis of different environmental issues, *Malayala Manorama* (48) and *Deshabhimani* (48) gave equal number of items followed by *The Hindu* (46) and *Mangalam* (46) in terms of frequency of news items. However *Kerala Kaumudi* (22) allocated less frequency of items as compared to other news items. In the break-up of coverage given to different news items, solid/hazardous waste disposal got more coverage in all seven newspapers in comparison to other news items (Table 65).

Table–65
Frequency of Environmental News under Different Subject Categories: Newspaper-wise

	Newspaper						
Subject Categories	*Malayala Manorama*	*Mathrubhumi*	*Deshabhimani*	*Kerala Kaumudi*	*Mangalam*	*The New Indian Express*	*The Hindu*
Environmental education	2	-	4	2	4	2	10
Climate change	4	-	8	-	-	4	10
Sand mining	-	4	4	2	-	-	2
Agriculture	6	8	4	6	4	2	4
Solid/hazardous waste disposal	16	14	14	8	18	14	6
Drinking water pollution	2	4	-	-	2	-	-
River pollution	10	8	8	2	12	4	8
Government initiative	8	4	6	2	6	4	6
Total	48	42	48	22	46	30	46

In terms of coverage in each city, Kozhikode (96) obtained more coverage of environmental issues followed by Kochi (84), Kottayam (52) and Thiruvananthapuram (50). Further, in terms of coverage given to different environmental issues, solid/

hazardous waste got more coverage in Kozhikode whereas river pollution got more coverage in Kochi. However, in Kottayam two categories of news items, agriculture and drinking water pollution did not get any coverage while drinking water pollution did not get any coverage in Thiruvananthapuram (Table 66).

Table–66
Frequency of Environmental News under Different Subject Categories: City-wise

	City			
Subject Categories	*Thiruvananthapuram*	*Kottayam*	*Kochi*	*Kozhikode*
Environmental education	6	4	2	12
Climate change	10	8	6	2
Sand mining	4	2	2	4
Agriculture	6	–	18	10
Solid/hazardous waste	8	22	24	36
Drinking water pollution	–	–	2	6
River pollution	10	8	30	4
Government initiative	6	8	–	22
Total	50	52	84	96

Thiruvananthapuram

In the coverage given to different subject categories by seven newspapers, it was found that none of the newspapers gave any coverage to drinking water pollution while two newspapers, *Malayala Manorama* and *The Hindu* allocated two news items each to environmental education. Further, *Deshabhimani* covered sand mining issues by giving two news items during the study period (Table 67).

Table–67
Thiruvananthapuram: Distribution of Frequency of Environmental News Items Under Different Subject Categories in Select Dailies

Subject Categories	*Newspaper*						
	Malayala Mano-rama	*Mathru-bhumi*	*Desha-bhimani*	*Kerala Kau-mudi*	*Mang-alam*	*The New Indian Express*	*The Hindu*
Environmental education	2	-	-	-	-	-	4
Climate change	2	-	2	-	-	2	4
Sand mining	-	-	4	-	-	-	-
Agriculture	-	-	2	2	-	-	2
Solid/hazardous waste disposal	-	2	-	-	2	4	-
Drinking water pollution	-	-	-	-	-	-	-
River pollution	-	2	-	-	4	2	2
Government initiative	-	-	2	-	2	2	-
Total	4	4	10	2	8	10	12

Kottayam

In Kottayam city, agriculture and drinking water pollution did not receive any coverage in all the dailies, whereas six dailies covered solid/hazardous waste news items while *Mathrubhumi* did not cover the subject category. Three newspapers *Malayala Manorama, Kerala Kaumudi* and *The New Indian Express* did not cover river pollution.

Kochi

In the analysis of newspapers, it was found that all the seven newspapers covered two subject categories, solid/hazardous waste disposal and river pollution. While none of the newspapers

Table–68
Kottayam: Distribution of Frequency of Environmental News Items Under Different Subject Categories in Select Dailies

Subject Categories	*Newspaper*						
	Malayala Manorama	*Mathrubhumi*	*Deshabhimani*	*Kerala Kaumudi*	*Mangalam*	*The New Indian Express*	*The Hindu*
Environmental education	-	-	-	-	2	-	2
Climate change	2	-	2	-	-	2	2
Sand mining	-	-	-	1	-	-	-
Agriculture	-	-	-	-	-	-	-
Solid/hazardous waste disposal	2	-	2	2	12	2	2
Drinking water pollution	-	-	-	-	-	-	-
River pollution	-	2	2	-	2	-	2
Government initiative	2	2	-	-	-	2	2
Total	6	4	6	3	16	6	10

dedicated any news items to government initiatives on environment. Although drinking water pollution was an important issue, *Malayala Manorama* allocated one news item to it. *Mathrubhumi* gave one news item on sand mining while *Mangalam* dedicated one news item to environment education.

Kozhikode

In terms of allocation of frequency of news item to different subject categories, sand mining was given one news item each by *Mathrubhumi* and *The Hindu*. When six newspapers covered solid/hazardous waste disposal news items, *Kerala Kaumudi* did not cover the subject category. Interestingly, agriculture subject category was covered by four newspapers viz., *Malayala*

Table–69
Kochi: Distribution of Frequency of Environmental News Items under Different Subject Categories in Select Dailies

	Newspaper						
Subject Categories	*Malayala Mano-rama*	*Mathru-bhumi*	*Desha-bhimani*	*Kerala Kau-mudi*	*Mang-alam*	*The New Indian Express*	*The Hindu*
Environmental education	-	-	-	-	2	-	-
Climate change	-	-	4	-	-	-	2
Sand mining	-	2	-	-	-	-	-
Agriculture	4	8	-	-	4	-	2
Solid/hazardous waste disposal	2	4	4	6	2	4	2
Drinking water pollution	2	-	-	-	-	-	-
River pollution	10	4	4	2	6	2	2
Government initiative	-	-	-	-	-	-	-
Total	16	18	12	8	14	6	8

Manorama, Deshabhimani, Kerala Kaumudi and *The New Indian Express*. The other three newspapers *Mathrubhumi, Mangalam* and *The Hindu* did not cover the subject category.

Table–70
Kozhikode: Distribution of Frequency of Environmental News Items Under Different Subject Categories in Select Dailies

Subject Categories	*Newspaper*						
	Malayala Mano-rama	*Mathru-bhumi*	*Desha-bhimani*	*Kerala Kau-mudi*	*Mang-alam*	*The New Indian Express*	*The Hindu*
Environment education	-	-	4	2	-	2	4
Climate change	-	-	-	-	-	-	2
Sand mining	-	2	-	-	-	-	2
Agriculture	2	-	2	4	-	2	-
Solid/hazardous waste disposal	12	8	8	-	2	4	2
Drinking water pollution	-	4	-	-	2	-	-
River pollution	6	-	2	-	-	-	2
Government initiative	-	2	4	2	4	-	4
Total	20	16	20	8	8	8	16

7
Case Studies

This chapter presents case studies with respondent journalists who are part of the sample for the study. Case study method was adopted to ascertain their educational background, perceptions on environment reporting in Kerala newspapers, coverage of specific environmental issues and problems they encounter while reporting environmental issues. The researcher also made an effort to ascertain information on their level of job satisfaction, relationship between the journalist and the management, between journalists and their sources, style of writing and the treatment of environmental stories in Kerala newspapers. The researcher spent nearly three to four hours with each journalist-respondent to ascertain his or her views. As the respondents have requested the researcher to maintain secrecy of their names, the researcher has not disclosed their names.

Case Study 1

Mr. H who is working as chief sub-editor in the popular Malayalam daily, *Malayala Manorama*, joined the daily as a trainee in July 1993. Being the youngest in the family, he had his education up to graduation in his village in Kerala. With science background in pre-degree course, Mr. H completed his graduation in Physics.

During his graduation, he was closely associated with the student wing of the Left movement and also the Kerala Sastra

Sahitya Parishad (KSSP), a group which creates awareness on environmental issues. These activities oriented him more towards the profession of journalism and he obtained a Diploma in Journalism. Later on, he joined for the post-graduation course in Journalism and Mass Communication but discontinued due to personal reasons.

In 1993, one of the leading newspapers in Malayalam, *Malayala Manorama* advertised for the post of sub-editor trainee and Mr. H was selected. As it was the policy of the newspaper to train the selected journalists in one of the specialized fields, Mr. H opted for environment reporting. He was posted as a reporter in the northern district of Kannur, where the newspaper was launching its new edition. Entrusted with local reporting, he reported from this rural area on environmental issues. There was a major deforestation drive of mangrove forests in the name of converting the area for acqua farming to provide subsistence to the local people who returned from Kuwait after Iraqi invasion. However, the management refused to publish the stories that Mr. H had filed on deforestation. He said, "Some of the local people must have influenced the management."

In spite of moving to the desk as a sub-editor in 1995, Mr. H continued reporting on environmental issues. Two reports that he filed, one on China clay mining in the area and another story on a member of the judiciary who had manipulated evidence to support the interests of landlords in the area, were rejected by the editor even when they had depended on reliable sources. Mr. H said that the chief editor after going through these stories sent them back with a remark that "there are valid and truthful points" in the two stories but newspaper could not publish them as the people involved had close relation with the paper. Mr. H passed on the story of China clay mining to another newspaper, which published it with the by-line of a reporter and received the state award for the same. However, the story on member of the judiciary was not published by any of the newspapers. To his utter dismay, Mr. H found that all records that supported the story disappeared mysteriously from the treasury after his story was circulated in the newspaper offices. In May 1996, Mr. H was transferred to the Kottayam edition and was made the editor of the science desk. This was the time when his interest in environment took deeper roots. He made a study of major issues like global warming and plastic waste. During his editorship, environmental issues received wide coverage on the science page.

In 1998, he underwent a 45-day professional training on "environment in news" given by the Reuter Foundation with the consent of the management. The training conducted at the Greens' College of Oxford University was more practice oriented where even the daily classroom sessions had to be reported in news style. Mr. H submitted a feature on the millennium project at the Royal Botanical Garden at Kew in southwest London in England.

In 1999, Mr. H was again transferred to the edition at the industrial and business town of Kochi as senior sub-editor. Even though he was at the desk, whenever there was a serious environmental issue in the area, Mr. H was deputed to report on it. Mr. H said that management trusted his experience and knowledge in environment reporting. Severe carbon pollution in the nearby town of Ambalamugal was opposed by the local residents and they burnt the newspaper where Mr. H was working for not supporting them. The management asked Mr. H to visit the area to pacify the local people and to report their views in the newspaper in order to contain losing circulation in the area. Mr. H found that it took so much of time to convince them that the newspaper was with the people. Nevertheless, he prepared a five-day series on the issue including a human-interest story about a hospital that was converted into a bar. Along with the series of news items, newspaper also published press releases issued by the carbon company on the issue. After the first day of publication, company mounted pressure on Mr. H to change the version of the news. He objected. When they threatened him over phone, he told them to talk to the management if they had any contrary views. Further, the management did not talk to Mr. H but the newspaper stopped the series on the third day. Disgusted, Mr. H passed on the remaining information to another daily, which published it. He affirmed that all through his career as an environmental reporter, he saw to it that news stories he had prepared on any serious social issue should get reported in any of the newspaper, small or big, if his newspaper declined to publish them.

The Green Peace Foundation wanted to make a study of selected ecological hotspots of the world and the industrial belt of Kerala was one among them. Mr. H passed on the necessary information on the pollution in the area. In this context, he supported the continuation of Hindustan Insecticides Limited (HIL) in the area but argued that company cannot shy away from installing the necessary infrastructure to control the pollution.

Mr. H is of the view that today, newspapers in Kerala are increasingly becoming sensational. Even in the case of environmental news, he observed that newspapers prioritize only the news that grabs the attention of the readers. All issues are not reported. "The amount of reporting done has failed to develop the political will in solving various issues", he said. Mr. H opines that most of the environmental stories are "compromised" under corporate pressure. He is of the opinion that the controversial eviction of hill resorts at Munnar major hill station in Kerala in 2007 was abruptly stopped because of the corporate pressure. "Both the newspapers and the Government are influenced." For instance, Mr. H points out that a major water theme park in Kochi was found to pollute the nearby rivers. In protest, the members of the Panchayat conducted a press conference where reporters of all the newspapers and TV channels attended. Yet, none of them carried the news item, as the management of the water theme park was one of their main advertisers. Further, he says that newspapers alone cannot create environmental awareness by reporting. "There has to be a political will", he concluded.

Case Study 2

Mr. A has worked in five English dailies during his journalism career spanning nearly 22 years. In 1976, after completing his school, Mr. A came to Kerala from Karnataka for his college education. During Emergency (1975-77) he was influenced by the extreme leftist ideologies. Being very active in student politics, he used to conduct study classes for the party workers. After completing his graduation in Economics and post-graduation in English literature, Mr. A desired to be a teacher like his father. As a result of frequent travels into the forest areas with his friends, environment became a part of his life during the period.

In 1985, the English daily, *Indian Express* advertised for the post of trainee journalist and Mr. A was selected for the post. Initially, he was hesitant to go for reporting as his request to be made an environmental or sports reporter was not accepted. He observed that there was no concept of environmental reporting during that time. After two years of training, Mr. A was not given a permanent post on the ground that he did not pass the typewriting exam. Frustrated, he quit the job in 1986 and left for Mumbai to become a journalist. There he moved from one newspaper to the other, and finally he opted for the desk job in the English daily, *The Times of India*. The Silent Valley issue was threatening the environment of Kerala during that time. Mr. A was asked to report on the issue, which appeared with his by-line and was highly appreciated by readers and also by the resident editor. Thereafter he reported major environmental issues in Kerala for the paper.

Subsequently, Mr. A was desperate to return to Kerala, as he preferred to have a life in his native state rather than moving into big cities in the north to build up a career. In 1989, he was back to *Indian Express* where he had worked initially but was posted in Bangalore. By 1992, he was transferred to the Kochi unit in Kerala as senior sub-editor. There he learnt the perfect art of editing. However, his ambition to be an environmental reporter was never accepted and hence avoided to be a reporter.

In 1995, sensing that business reporting was gaining importance, he moved to the *Financial Express* as chief sub-editor. Mr. A continued to report environmental issues for the newspaper, putting them in suitable contexts for a business paper. Further, Mr. A informed that the newspaper preferred his environmental stories to have a poetic intro. Most of the direct reports used to get rejected. Stories from the south remained in the southern edition and never made it to the main page of the paper. In 1997, he became the deputy news editor and soon went on to become the news editor of the edition. In 2000, the paper closed down its Kerala edition and asked Mr. A to move to Mumbai to co-ordinate the bureau and deskwork. However, when he insisted to be in Kerala, he was made special correspondent of the paper in Kerala. He said that he had a better chance to report environmental issues in the financial newspaper than in *Indian Express*. As the circulation of the paper started going down, he started looking for a business paper with a better reach. Thus in February 2007, he moved on to be the special correspondent for *Mint,* the business daily of *Hindustan Times.*

As an environmental reporter, he used to follow the environmental issues in-depth, while discussing them with fellow journalists in other newspapers to set an agenda for reporting issues of relevance. However, he opined that in view of competition among newspapers, some of the newspapers now try to maintain confidentiality of the profession. He expressed the view that there has to be better cooperation and goodwill among newspapers to fight for a social cause like environment. He said, "New breed of journalists are behind money, fame and power. Principles and commitment make the difference in environmental reporting and that quality is lacking now and hence newspapers don't make an impact".

He also said, "In environmental reporting, fieldwork is important as reliable sources are less". He used to study extensively the research material available on various issues and consult experts. He is of the opinion that environmental awareness among newspaper readers in Kerala is high as debates and discussions are part of life. "Newspapers have played a great role in maintaining this high level of awareness. Today's generation is better aware of conservation of environment especially in the case of issues like urban waste including plastic," he said.

He said that reporting environmental issues cannot be avoided as information on such topics are major requirements for the readers in Kerala and unless "you give what is necessary for the readers, circulation will fall". However, in relation to investigative stories about environmental issues, he said that the content in environmental reports was not satisfactory. Mr. A observed that advertisement personnel are given prominent place in newspaper organizations as they bring revenue for the paper, and journalists in the newspaper are relegated to back-seat.

Case Study 3

Mr. S working as bureau chief and also as special correspondent in the popular Malayalam daily *Mathrubhumi* has completed 32 years of service in the profession. His journalistic career began as a freelance reporter for the fortnightly *Youth Times* of *The Times of India.*

Having obtained his post-graduation degree in History from Maharaja's College in Kochi, Mr. S was closely associated with social activities. His uncle, being a prominent leader of the rationalist movement, was the publisher of a rationalist magazine in Malayalam. He appointed him as a translator of articles from English for the magazine. As a pre-degree student, he translated 20 pages of Pundit Jawaharlal Nehru's speech on new social order and education for publication in the magazine.

Mr. S's association with the present newspaper began when he was visiting the office to submit articles written by his uncle for publication in the newspaper at the Kochi office. In the process, he was introduced to the bureau chief of the unit and was entrusted campus reporting for the paper as a freelancer without any salary. Eventually, this led him to general reporting. In 1975, Mr. S became the campus reporter for the *Youth Times* of *The Times of India*. During this period, Mr. S translated some of the famous works of the Japanese filmmaker Akira Kuruzova into Malayalam upon request from the noted filmmaker of Kerala, Adoor Gopalakrishnan. In 1977, he joined United News of India (UNI), the national news agency, as a reporter temporarily. This helped him establish contacts with many people and in the process developed sources in the state and central cabinet. Further, he understood the importance of sources and the mutual trust that should exist between a reporter and the source. Also, he understood that even a junior reporter like him could establish contacts at all levels.

In 1978, he joined *Veekshanam,* a prominent Malayalam daily, on a permanent basis. The newspaper was considered the mouthpiece of the ruling political party at that time. He feared a clash of interest with the management on political issues. However, he had to compromise expecting a good exposure in the profession. In the initial days, he was given the court beat. Because of the experience already gained in the profession since his college days, he found the beat interesting. He vividly remembers reporting and interviewing the rescued captain of a wrecked foreign ship off the Arabian coast. The Indian Navy had rescued the crew and through his contacts Mr. S gained access to report the event. The exclusive report appeared only in the newspaper he was working for the then bureau chief and the editor of the present newspaper noticed this scoop. Under strong recommendation from the bureau chief, he joined the newspaper in March 1980. Once again he was asked to do court beat.

In September 1980, he was assigned to report the eviction of tribal people by the government who had encroached into one of the evergreen forests of Kerala. This trip influenced him to develop interest in environmental issues especially related to the conservation of forestland. During 1982-86, he visited forest areas with the help of forest range officers and studied in-depth about trees, the wild animals, life in the forest, the tribals and so on. As a result, he extensively reported in the newspaper and in the magazine section of the newspaper.

During 1988, he travelled to various parts of Madhya Pradesh, Rajasthan, Delhi and in 1989, had been to the Himalayas. During 1993-96, he was promoted as special reporter and was posted to Delhi. In 1997, he was posted to the Calicut edition of the paper. In 1998, he was at the Kochi edition. From 1999-2001, he worked at Calicut once again. Since 2002, he is at the Kochi office as special correspondent and bureau chief.

He vividly remembers a story that drew the attention of the then Prime Minister Mrs. Indira Gandhi. In 1983, there was a plan to develop a 20km. road inside the Silent Valley to develop tourism by the Forest Department and Kerala Tourism Development Corporation. Mr. S filed continuous stories on the ecological imbalance which will be created due to the project. Sahyadri Development Society, a local environment group, submitted a memorandum, which included Mr. S's story to the then Prime Minister. With the intervention of the Prime Minister, the project was abandoned.

In 1986, there was a threat to the evergreen hills of one of the national parks in Kerala and Mr. S, through his paper undertook a vigorous campaign and the project was given up. Further, in a wildlife sanctuary, some influential people wanted to destroy the sanctuary area by laying a road and a campaign by the newspaper resulted in the abandoning of the idea of laying of the road.

In his reporting on environmental issues, Mr. S said that he had enjoyed full freedom from the management. According to him, when he joined the profession, environmental awareness was very low among readers. The role newspapers could play in environmental awareness was first proved through the campaign against the Silent Valley project. A similar issue where newspapers could show its strength was the issue at Plachimada, where Coca Cola Company was depleting the ground water level by massive usage for its manufacturing plant.

While reporting on environmental issues, Mr. S used to repeatedly check information with the experts. He feels that direct reporting is more impressive in environmental reporting and that any other style would make it lose its importance. He said, "An environmental reporter should have a vision about what he is trying to achieve through his reports. He should feel the pulse of the people. Nature clubs and environmental education at the school level have gone a long way in creating awareness and newspapers should join such efforts for better results". In Kerala, where literacy rate is high, people are now conscious about the various hazards that arise out of destruction of the environment and "the newspapers need to influence the government to take action". He observes that newspapers today campaign more on political issues than environmental issues and he feels that the journalists are over-burdened with work as they undertake all beats. He also expressed the view that environment requires a beat. He observes that in Kerala, where newspaper reading is a daily habit, government will not be able to neglect environmental issues that appear in newspapers. Kerala newspapers do cover environmental issues extensively compared to other regional dailies in other states. However, political consciousness is needed for these reports to make an impact, he concludes.

Case Study 4

Mr. V who is currently working as news editor in one of the editions of *Deshabhimani* newspaper has completed 27 years in the profession. Influenced by the thoughts of Leftist movement, during the school days, he was the speaker of the school parliament; a post fiercely fought and won through the school elections based on politics.

Mr. V was active in politics and was the leader of the Farm Labourers' Association in his district. He used to organize the labourers of the area to fight for their rights and attended the classes of senior Left party leaders. As the party was running a newspaper, it used to recruit young party workers with a literary background to work for the newspaper. Thus in 1979, Mr. V who was on the look-out for a job was asked to join the newspaper. Mr. V started his career as a proof-reader on daily wages.

In due course of time, Mr. V became a reporter and sub-editor and served many editions. During the initial years, he worked as a reporter and was extremely enthusiastic as he found that his views were published without any editing. He says that it is the case in most of the newspapers as the newspapers select trainee journalists who have a mindset suiting the policy of the newspaper. Therefore, the reporter seems to enjoy total freedom.

When he was at Kozhikode, there was an issue of scavengers being forced to collect and carry the night soil to dumping sites. It was the belief of the people in the area that modern toilets should not be used. Because there was a definite need to change the attitude of the people, newspapers in the area took up a massive campaign aimed at bringing a psychological change in the people. Soon it became a mass movement when prominent leaders joined the campaign. Over a period of time, the area became free of pollution and stink of the night soil. A similar campaign by newspapers at local level was the one at Trichur. A large number of small industries producing sponge iron were polluting the air, water and the agriculture fields near Trichur town. Campaign by the local editions of the newspapers made people in the area come together to fight against the pollution. As a result some of the companies were forced to close down and others adhered to safety measures to prevent pollution, Mr. V said.

However he says that such success is limited for newspaper campaigns unless a research organization takes up the issue. He cited the example of pollution in the Eloor industrial belt of Kerala where crops in the field had been dying because of the gas emissions. He observed that although newspapers reported the issue, there was no agency to do the necessary research to tell the newspapers what follow up can be done about the issue.

He says that development is required and that there is no mistake in newspapers supporting development. Development is not possible without adversely affecting the environment. He says that environment will keep changing. He feels that the newspapers should report on the concept of environmental management instead of accusing the authorities. "Reporters don't realize the reason for environmental problems", he said.

He expressed the view that newspapers should realize that citizens have a larger role to play in saving the environment and should project stories in such a way that they will result in citizen action. But he admits that if newspapers write from such an angle, readers may not like such news. He said that newspapers could not make a campaign on serious issues like spreading of epidemic fever during the last two years in several districts of Kerala and affect of pesticides on food items because of lack of in-depth analysis. In the case of deaths due to mysterious fever recently, the newspapers were unable to report even the exact number of people who died because of the fever.

According to him, while reporting on environmental issues, journalist receives contradicting viewpoints from different sources. It's the duty of the journalists to judge what is right and what is wrong and this is a highly demanding job. Reporter too may be wrong in judgment and then the news editor can give a better judgment. However, even the newspaper has a policy and the journalists including the news editor will be forced to adhere to it. He says that the newspapers in Kerala are adopting a trend where they prefer to generate panic in the minds of the people by reporting on environmental issues.

Case Study 5

Mrs. P has completed 30 years of journalistic career working in two of the most popular English dailies in Kerala. Born in Malaysia, she completed her schooling in Malaysia and later on in Kerala. Her maternal grandfather who was a Sanskrit scholar was writing the leader for one of the oldest Malayalam dailies. Inspired by him, she pursued the Diploma in Journalism course conducted by an institute in Trivandrum as soon as she completed her graduation in English in 1975. Simultaneously, she continued her post-graduation in English literature.

In 1977, the English daily *Indian Express* advertised for the post of trainee journalist. She applied and was selected after a long process. Eventually, she joined the newspaper at the Kochi edition as a trainee journalist with a monthly stipend of Rs. 300. After two years, she joined the desk as sub-editor. In the initial days, she was editing letters to the editor and helped the chief sub-editor in sorting out and selecting the agency copy in addition to her editing work. Soon she was entrusted with the job of writing features for the paper.

During the next 23 years of her career in the newspaper, she specialized in feature writing and covered a variety of topics. Environment was one of the main areas as she had interest in the subject. More than issues of environmental conflict in the area, she concentrated more on general environmental topics like rain harvesting, organic farming etc. She said that she could not cover several environmental conflict news, as she was not working on the news reporting. When the serious issue of ground water depletion due to the massive planting of acacia trees in the city came to light, she conducted a major campaign against it. Other newspapers also took up the issue and as a result acacia trees plantation was stopped through a major drive.

As a feature writer, her analyses became a regular column on the opinion page of the newspaper where she wrote on all major environmental issues of regional, national and international importance. In due course, she became chief sub-editor and was moved to the main desk. Here she was put on night shifts as well. Slowly difference in opinion with the senior editors took place and she started distancing herself from the newspaper. In 2001, she quit the paper and joined *The Hindu*, another English national daily where she joined as senior sub-editor. Within a year, she became the chief sub-editor and later became the in-charge of the weekly pull out.

Because of her interest in environmental issues, she is keen on reporting important issues. However, these issues do not occupy prominent place in the pull out unless they are important. She says even though "compartmentalization" of news is good for accountability to news stories, she personally likes to handle all subjects of importance and does not want to be labelled as a particular beat reporter. Though specialization is very important, an environmental reporter may end up desperate for environmental issues to report. She feels that lack of reliable sources and correct information always pose a problem in environmental reporting. For instance, she had filed a story on the e-waste, which she feels is a major environmental threat in the coming years. She found that no information technology company in Kerala had the clear idea of what to do with the e-waste. Statistics were hard to find. She says newspapers will not campaign for it until it becomes a serious issue. Nevertheless it was a story, which received good response.

In relation to women journalists, she says that most of them report on general issues and very few specialize on environment. She says that newspapers in Kerala are keeping a vigil on the social issues when compared to newspapers in other states. But there can be more issue based reporting. Issues like drinking water problem are expected to receive more space. Every social activity in Kerala is increasingly becoming commercialized. So is the newspaper. She feels that news is slanted. "A reader can predict how a newspaper will report an issue. It's like reading a fiction. One can enjoy while reading the content of a news item. Previously this was not the trend. The division in opinion between the newspapers on issues was not as well drawn as it is now. Newspapers are not working towards creating a change. She says that so much is being written about certain issues and beyond a point one feels ashamed that there is no impact", she concludes.

Case Study 6

Mr. B born in a Muslim family in a village in one of the northern districts of Kerala was the first generation member from the family to attend to a college for education. With the support of his mother who had a progressive outlook, he obtained post-graduate degree in Economics.

Being a regular newspaper reader, he subscribed to an English newspaper. During his college days, he was associated with the environment related activities of Kerala Sastra Sahitya Parishad (KSSP) and used to travel frequently. In 1980, he secured a job in the gramin bank in his village. With the desire to be a journalist, even though he did not know anything about the profession, he quit the bank job after one year. Due to financial constraints, he took up part-time teaching in a college, in order to continue his studies. Further, he accidentally came across the notification in a newspaper for the Bachelor course in Journalism offered by the Calicut University. He joined and completed the course.

In 1984, he was selected as a trainee journalist in two regional newspapers. As one was branded as a religious newspaper he stayed away from it and joined the other. On account of a good library in the newspaper office, he could read many books and magazines on a regular basis. Meanwhile, *Indian Express* selected him as a trainee journalist. After the training, in 1985, he was posted at Vijayawada as a sub-editor trainee with a monthly stipend of Rs. 750. Initially he looked after the art and film review sections. By 1987, he was transferred to the Kochi office and within a year was transferred to Chennai. He was in Chennai for five years where he first worked as a sub-editor and then as a reporter.

In 1993, he shifted to *The Hindu* national daily as a senior sub-editor. By 1995, he came to Kerala and joined the Kochi unit as a senior reporter. There he chose to specialize in environment reporting as part of the social reporting beat. He vividly remembers an investigative story he did on a non-governmental organization (NGO) that had enacted an encroachment drama in a forest with a group of tribals in the area. The tribals were assured 'pattayam' (a title deed) on the encroached land they occupied after collecting Rs. 2000 from them. They were made to pose for photographs in the encroached land. Within days, when the police evicted them, the eviction proceedings were also photographed by the NGO to register a case against the eviction. Sensing foul play, Mr. B and the cameraman travelled into the forest and posed as local people from the nearby town. Further, they gathered information from key figures and a series of investigative reports were published which finally exposed the foul play of the NGO. He believes in verifying information while filing reports on environmental issues. "Value addition" to the news report is done through experts' comments.

He received three state awards for his reports out of which one story was on the issue of drinking water problem in the city because of the construction of a national stadium in the heart of the city. He also received the Sarojini Naidu award at the national level for reporting on the changes that have come into the lives of Muslim women owing to 33 per cent reservation for women in politics. As a senior reporter, he could travel across the state to report on environmental issues from anywhere. Reports on pollution of Periyar river and felling of teakwood in agency areas of Idukki district received wide attention from the authorities to initiate action on the issues. He believes that newspapers' job is to get the environmental issues to the spotlight. He observed that many environmental issues in remote areas might go unnoticed because most of the reporters are urban-based. Being a reporter of a national daily, he got a rapport with sources as multi-sourcing is extremely important in environmental reporting.

In 2000, Mr. B visited Germany as part of the Group Study Exchange (GSE) programme to study about the culture and traditions of German people. In the same year, he became the principal correspondent and by 2003 was elevated to the post of special correspondent. In 2003, he was selected for the one-year Fulbright Fellowship to study "newsroom management" in the University of Maryland, Washington. He observed the working style in the newsrooms of major newspapers like *New York Times, Los Angeles Times, Washington Post, Washington Times* and *Times* magazine. He received one-year membership in the National Press Club, Washington where he could attend press conferences held by world leaders. The training helped him in having a better understanding of reporting including observing their style of reporting environmental issues as well.

Case Study 7

Born in a business family in a small town in the central Travancore area of Kerala, Mr. J is at present the deputy editor of *Mathrubhumi* having completed 38 years of service in the profession. Mr. J was actively involved in political and literary activities during his school and college days. After completing graduation in Physics in 1967, he obtained Diploma in Journalism from an institute in Trivandrum. He joined the present newspaper as an internee and later became a suburban reporter in 1970 in Ernakulam, one of the towns in Kerala. During Emergency (1975-77) in the country, reporters had very little choice to report on political issues and they had to focus on developmental issues. As part of it, Mr. J had the chance to report on environmental issues. He observed that environmental issues were difficult to report as there was no possibility of training for journalists at that time.

During that period, people living near the paddy fields of Kuttanad described as the rice bowl of the state were facing major health problems. Local people were suffering from itching, eye irritation and vision problems. Moreover, there was lot of panic in the area when newspapers started reporting on the issue. A few research agencies found that extensive use of fertilizers in the area for the crops polluted the air, food and even the water. Slowly newspapers campaigned about the pollution, which resulted in creating awareness among the people. Eventually, they started taking necessary precautions to avoid a catastrophe and they attempted better farming methods.

Mr. J moved to the desk as senior sub-editor in 1984 and continued to move up the career at regular intervals during his posting in various editions. When there was a leakage of ammonia gas from one of the fertilizer plants in the Ellor industrial belt of Kerala, there was wide newspaper coverage. Photographs represented the horror of the mishap as residents started running helter-skelter leaving their homes on account of a fear of a major tragedy like Bhopal. They presented the alarming situation better than news reports and a campaign by the newspapers forced various industries in the area to install pollution control measures. In these two incidents, Mr. J was involved in reporting the issues.

He opines that amount of environmental reporting in Kerala newspapers is satisfactory. However, Kerala newspapers are undergoing a sea change in their content owing to changes taking place in the society. "Truly, politics always is the major focus. Nevertheless, a luxurious lifestyle is slowly creeping into the Kerala society and newspapers are forced to carry information on fashion, food habits and business", he said.

Because of these trends, newspapers fear that the readers will boycott the paper if their demands are not met with. According to him, a new trend has come up recently. The space for obituary news is slowly increasing beyond one page in regional papers. Certain newspapers are bought because of the number of obituary news it carries. Therefore, serious environmental reporting to give authentic information on various environmental issues affecting the lives of the people is declining. For example, he says, the seasonal mysterious fever that was appearing in certain parts of the state along with varied figures of death toll reported every day by different newspapers received criticism from the readers. Contrary to the popular belief that readers do not read serious news is proved immensely wrong in Kerala. According to him, readership will be there for such issues that are affecting the lives of people and are taken seriously by the people.

Further, he adds that money is an important factor in tackling the environmental issues. There is threat for the life of the reporter who goes for reporting issues like sand mining where large amount of money is at stake by the mafia. He says that even if the newspaper reports on sand mining, it can be controlled only if the authorities really wish to. But as sand mining comes as a source of revenue for the panchayat, they will never interfere. He says, "Environmental reporting can be made more effective under the supervision of a team of journalists. However, no such elaborate set up exists in Kerala newspapers and the newspaper cannot afford to have a journalist especially for the environmental beat when the readership for such news items is low. Thus seriousness in environmental reporting goes down."

He opines that environmental reporting in Kerala doesn't have the much needed transparency and they have short-term goals while reporting on various issues. He says that newspapers highlight the construction of flats in the city while reporting about the lowering ground water level.

He says that advertisement pressure is a reality but should be dealt with while reporting sensitive issues. He says that his newspaper could take up the challenge of avoiding advertisements by multinational companies while taking up the campaign against the threat by the cool drink unit of a multinational company. Even then, the newspaper survived and won the appreciation of readers. He says that whenever newspapers have raised public opinion about an issue, there has been a positive impact. However, such a campaign cannot be done unless the issue is affecting daily lives of the people.

Mr. J prefers a narrative style while reporting on environmental issues. He says that his newspaper is a 'reporters' newspaper and gives total freedom for the reporter. He says that checking is not an important criterion when you are reporting something true. He says that newspaper should not have any "hidden agenda" regarding an issue. If the reporter is alert, no bias can get into his report. He agrees to the fact that there are high chances of an environment reporter falling into controversies.

According to him, journalism is becoming a profession with large number of awards attached for merit. However, unhealthy competition exists among newspapers to receive an award and such an attitude is dangerous. He says that personally he was never interested in awards and that they made no difference to his commitment to the profession. He says that environmental reporting is not a recognized beat in Kerala newspapers. Also, as the number of editions goes on increasing, the environmental news items are becoming more and more localized and hence a larger relevance is curtailed, in the context of the entire state.

Case Study 8

Mr. O, born into a family of teachers, wanted to be a journalist although his family members insisted him to become a teacher. He completed his post-graduation in English literature in 1985. Because of his liking for the wild life since childhood, he used to read and understand the literature related to it. He used to trek through the forests and hills. In 1987, having completed a Diploma course in Journalism after post-graduation, he joined *Malayala Manorama* as a trainee journalist. After one year, he was sent as a reporter to Idukki, one of the remote districts of Kerala. His was a one-member bureau and had to do all jobs including collection of money from the newspaper agents and maintaining their accounts. As the district covered large amount of forest areas and hill ranges, he could report extensively on issues relating to environment.

His first extensive story on wild life was prepared during the training period. As the senior sub-editor didn't want to give him a by-line during the training period, it was withheld. It was published the very next day after completion of his training period. Thereafter, a series of reports on environmental issues related to forests were published. He informs that his commitment to nature made him look specifically for environmental issues. He says that most of the time management asked him to go for reporting. However, at times, he had to go on leave and then report on the issues. He remembers that the encroachment into one of the evergreen forests of the state and related issues were covered during that period.

According to him, the general notion that environment journalist is threatened during their work is wrong. He observes that people involved in environmental conflicts are not scared of newspaper reports. In his experience, people who try to fiddle more with the reports are the politicians who intend to get things reported in their favour.

In respect of sources, there are of two types of sources existing for him. First kind exists at a personal level and is more reliable. The other develops because of professionalism. They exist only as long as he continues in the profession. In his newspaper, if the environment report is against the editorial policy of the management, it is rejected. For instance, he submitted a report on the issue of a man selling the encroached government land from where he had been evicted. As the newspaper management had close links with that person, it did not publish the story. Another instance was the issue of growing special kind of tea plantations in lands that were developed for the purpose of business. Huge advertisements were given by the landowners for the purpose of teak plantations with the assurance that when these trees would be sold when they matured and the money thus accrued would be shared. Many invested in such plantations. Upon investigation, Mr. O found that the offer was not genuine as it had severe legal implications and also it was un-scientific to cut off teak trees before they attain maturity. He filed two stories, but they were not published. He says that reporters in small newspapers have better freedom to report environment issues but their readership is less. As newspapers prosper, their vested interests also prosper correspondingly.

As per Mr. O's observation, journalists in Kerala have a good rapport with each other. The tough competition between newspapers has not disturbed the cordial relationship between journalists. In the case of environmental issues, Mr. O is not very particular that his report has to be published in his own newspaper. If an objection is made to his report during a meeting, he will inform his seniors that the story is going to be published in other newspapers and it has happened many times. Over the years, he has understood the nature of his management. In case if he is keen on publishing it in his paper he files the report with a remark "vested interests" will obstruct the process of development or they destroy the environment. He finds tactics like this has often met with a positive response and these are the ways by which a reporter can influence the senior editorial team.

According to him, even the senior journalists are unable to understand the importance of certain environmental news items, as they are not aware of the importance of the subject. Once he suggested about a news item for publishing in the newspaper. The item occupied eight-page space in *Nature,* the international weekly journal of science. However, the matter got its place in the inside page as a box item in his paper. He says that environmental reporting needs good legwork and basic information should not go wrong even if concerned authorities provide wrong information or the report has to be filed at short notice. For instance, he says that it is essential for any reporter to make out the difference between a leopard and a tiger or what maximum length can a king cobra attain. He says that specialization in subjects like environment can improve reporting in Kerala newspapers. He agrees that there is difficulty in using the right language to report certain issues like industrial pollution. He is of the view that space given for environmental reporting is sufficient in the newspapers. According to him one cannot fill the entire newspaper with environmental news.

According to him, government does take serious note of news reports and takes action on them. Politicians are accountable to the voters. He says that newspapers also need to have a social auditing and a method has to be devised to put it into action. He is happy that there is a growing awareness among politicians about environment. He says that environment has been receiving a mention in the election manifesto in the last two elections and that it is a welcome move. He says that journalists are accountable only to the management for their salary and the statement that journalists are accountable to their readers is only a 'mockery'. A journalist will report what the management asks him or her to do even if it is against his or her wish. He says that when journalist does environmental reporting, it should be appreciated, as it is tempting for the journalist to specialize in subjects like politics or sports, which have a wider readership and hence can get recognition.

8

Summary and Conclusions

The industrial revolution transformed the way of life as people flocked to cities to work in factories. The earlier dependence of people on agriculture slowly shifted to industry, which increasingly affected the environment. Forests were cleared to provide wood for new buildings and paper products. Larger amounts of minerals were extracted from the earth for industrial purposes, and water use increased accordingly. Pollution, the by-product of industry, became one of the biggest problems, resulting in the destruction of nature. Coupled with these changes, the burgeoning population too contributed to the 'eco-catastrophe.' Brown (2003: 1) calls the earth a "planet under stress" with a "civilization in trouble." With the enormous destruction of the nature, the humanity at large is increasingly facing the following problems (Chattopadhyay and Franke, 2006: 7):

- global warming;
- impending water shortages;
- declining area and declining yields of productive land;
- pollution of land, fresh water, sea water and air; and
- biodiversity loss.

Historically, many nations which became independent after the Second World War in Asia, Africa and Latin America moved towards adopting the western style of industrialized development. Large and small-scale industries that were set up as part of development agenda adversely affected the environment (Murthy, 2000: 13). The development projects recommended by the experts had their own consequences both intended and unintended. For example, new varieties of seeds associated with the green revolution of the late 1960s in India increased the yield of foodgrain, reduced hunger and eliminated famine in the country as the intended consequence. The unintended consequence was that the new seed varieties required extensive use of chemical fertilizers, which polluted the water resources (Murthy, 2006: 13). Thus, environment and development became two sides of the same coin (Sawant, 1993: 78). Since the process of development cannot be stopped, damage to the environment can only be abated. Because of the mounting environmental problems, the quality of life is also being affected. In this context, United Nations Conference of World Leaders on Human Environment at Stockholm in 1972 known as the first Earth Summit paved the way for discussions and debates on environment-related issues. Scholars pointed out that public education is one of the key responsibilities of the media to create awareness among the politicians, bureaucrats, citizens, and other stakeholders by widely disseminating environmental information. The media can frame issues while setting an agenda.

In India, Kerala was the first state to achieve the highest literacy level of its people and widespread reading of newspapers led to the highest newspaper consumption in the country (Franke and Chasin, 1992: 53). Because newspaper reading is high in the state, if newspapers cover environmental issues adequately, it is expected to impact the readers. As journalists are considered mass educators, their role in educating the masses is very important. In this context, the perceptions of journalists working in seven broadsheet dailies located in four cities of Kerala viz., the *Malayala Manorama, Mathrubhumi, Deshabhimani, Kerala Kaumudi, Mangalam, The New Indian Express* and *The Hindu*, published from four cities- Thiruvananthapuram, Kottayam, Kochi, and Kozhikode are examined in relation to the coverage of environmental issues in the state. The specific objectives of the study are:

1. To examine the socio-demographic profile of journalists in the sample study;
2. To ascertain the professional obligations of the journalists with regard to coverage of environmental issues;
3. To find out journalists' perception of coverage of environmental issues by Kerala newspapers;
4. To ascertain journalists' perception of accountability while reporting on environment and how journalists rely on identifying sources for environmental reporting;
5. To examine the problems faced by journalists while covering environmental issues;
6. To analyze the coverage given to environmental issues by the select dailies in terms of frequencies of news items; and finally
7. To offer suggestions to improve the coverage of environmental issues and also reporting of these issues in Kerala dailies.

Research Design

Keeping in view the objectives of the study, two research methods were used to collect data: survey method to collect data from the respondents and content analysis to obtain data about the coverage of environmental issues from the select dailies.

Survey Method

A survey method was used to collect data from the respondents who are working as journalists in seven newspapers published from the four cities. The universe of the study consisted of journalists working in seven broadsheet dailies published from four cities. The criterion for a journalist to be included in the sample was that he or she must have a minimum experience of 5 years.

In order to prepare the universe of the study, the researcher obtained data about the total number of journalists working in each newspaper from the respective newspaper offices. Once the total number of journalists working in each newspaper office was obtained, the names of journalists were arranged in alphabetical order for each city. Lists were thus prepared and more than 30 per cent of the journalists were randomly selected from seven newspapers in each city. Out of the total universe of 466 journalists, a total of 178 journalists were administered the questionnaire keeping in view the non-response and invalid questionnaires. Out of 178 questionnaires, 16 questionnaires were found to be invalid. A total of 162 questionnaires remained for final analysis.

Data Collection Instrument

Data collection instrument was a structured questionnaire, which included close-ended and open-ended questions relevant to the study. Part I of the questionnaire dealt with the identification data of respondents such as age, gender, education, income, working experience and so on. Part II contained questions relevant to professional obligations such as about profession of journalism, environmental reporting, sources of information, and types of risks involved in environmental reporting and so on. Part III consisted of questions relating to newspaper coverage of environmental issues such as quality of environmental reporting, training for journalists and others. Part IV included questions dealing with perception of journalists on specific environmental issues, role of newspapers in environmental issues etc.

Data Collection Procedure

The data pertaining to the study were collected between September and December 2006. The researcher visited the newspaper offices and requested the respondents to fill the structured questionnaire at their convenience. As the researcher is a native of Kerala, contacts were established with the respondents, who in turn introduced the researcher to other respondents. The researcher met the respondents in their offices for administering the questionnaire, and introduced herself as a former journalist and this made the respondent cooperate with the researcher. The researcher waited in the respective newspaper office as the respondent filled the questionnaire and sometimes the researcher explained the purpose of the study. It took nearly half an hour to one hour for the respondent to fill the questionnaire.

Content Analysis

In order to analyze the news contents of the seven selected dailies, content analysis technique was used. A total of 350 editions of the seven dailies covering four cities have been selected using constructed week and consecutive week sampling methods. Two subject categories, environment and others, were coded in terms of frequencies to ascertain the coverage given to environmental news by the seven dailies during the data collection period from the respondents i.e. September to December, 2006 (four months).

Major Findings

Out of 162 respondents who figured in the sample, a majority (21.6%) belonged to *Malayala Manorama* followed by *Mathrubhumi* (15.5%), *The Hindu* (14.1%) and *Deshabhimani* (14.1%). As much as 13 per cent belonged to *Kerala Kaumudi* and 11.2 per cent to *The New Indian Express* and 10.5 per cent to *Mangalam* daily (Table 7). Majority (30.2%) of the respondents are from Thiruvananthapuram followed by Kochi (25.9%), Kottayam (24.1%) and Kozhikode (19.8%) (Table 8). In respect of gender, majority (90.1%) were male journalists while the remaining were female journalists (9.9%) (Table 11).

Job Satisfaction

Out of the 162 respondents, 88.2 per cent respondents reported that they were satisfied with the employment while 3.7 per cent were not satisfied and 8.1 per cent reported that they couldn't say anything about the job. Job satisfaction was measured on a four-point scale: Very good, good, bad, very bad.

When asked about the reasons for job satisfaction, respondents reported seven different reasons for their job satisfaction. Nearly 64 per cent of the respondents reported good working environment for job satisfaction whereas nearly 19 per cent of the respondents cited job security as the reason for job satisfaction. 8.4 per cent of the respondents gave preference to comfortable salary whereas 4.2 per cent of the respondents opined that reporting subjects of interest was making them happy (Table 18). While 2.8 per cent of the respondents sighted freedom at work as the reason for their satisfaction, negligible percentage of 0.7 per cent gave organization's credibility for job satisfaction. Interestingly, 1.4 per cent reported political inclination as the reason for their job satisfaction. Overall, the duration of service and job satisfaction showed a strong negative correlation (r = -.65). Out of the six respondents who were not satisfied with their employment, three of them (50%) cited lack of job satisfaction as the reason. Others gave low salary, lack of support of management and lack of other opportunities as reasons (Table 20).

Professional Obligations

Out of 162 respondents in the sample a majority of 95.7 per cent believed that profession of journalism could help the society. However, 4.3 per cent was not sure about it. Regarding the respondents' perception of journalism profession, 47.7 per cent have reported that it can be used to create awareness among readers while 43.9 per cent reported that it could support peoples' cause. 8.4 per cent of the respondents expressed the view that it can make Government act on issues of concern (Table 21).

In relation to the coverage of environmental issues in the newspapers, 66.7 per cent of the respondents believed that newspapers in Kerala report environmental issues frequently. Nevertheless, 30.8 per cent of the respondents disagreed with this view while 2.5 per cent could not say anything.

When the respondents were asked to cite when environmental news appear in the Kerala newspapers, 68.5 per cent reported that they appear when an environmental issue surfaces (Table 23). About 29 per cent said that environmental reports appear more when there is an environmental conflict. However, two of the respondents said that environmental news appears because of vested interests. Interestingly, two respondents said that environmental news items appear when there is a lack of stories to publish.

Reasons for Environmental Issues

When asked about the main reason for environmental problems in Kerala, 48.8 per cent of the respondents cited man's indifference to environment as the reason while 30.9 per cent of the respondents reported lack of proper planning as the reason. Nearly 9 per cent of the respondents, however, gave industrialization as the reason while 2.4 per cent respondents cited political patronage and 1.2 per cent respondents felt lack of proper legal structure as the reason for environmental problems (Table 24).

Need for Environmental Journalist

A majority (91.9%) of the total respondents felt that newspapers in Kerala require a journalist to be on environmental beat. About 7 per cent of the respondents stated that there need not be a journalist only on environmental beat.

Asked whether it is difficult to cover environment, about 65 per cent reported that environmental reporting is not difficult to cover while 28.4 per cent of the respondents agreed that environmental coverage is difficult. Nearly 7 per cent of the respondents said they couldn't say whether it is difficult or not.

Frequency of Reporting by the Respondents

An attempt was made to assess the frequency of reporting of environmental issues by the respondents in the sample. It was measured on a three-point scale—less frequently, frequently and very frequently. Out of the 107 respondents who have reported, only 9.3 per cent of the respondents have reported very frequently followed by 37.4 per cent of the respondents who said that they have reported frequently and a close half of 53.3 per cent said that they have reported less frequently (Table 25). Among the 52 respondents who said that they had not reported environmental issues, 65.3 per cent reported that there is lack of opportunity to report whereas 21.2 per cent cited lack of time as the reason. Six respondents however said that they are unable to report though opportunity is there and one respondent reported that environmental issues are difficult to report (Table 27).

What do the journalists in Kerala newspapers think about the environmental beat? Out of the 162 respondents, 81.5 per cent of the respondents obtained professional satisfaction by reporting environmental issues. However, 5.6 per cent said that they don't receive any satisfaction and 12.9 per cent said they couldn't say whether there is satisfaction in environmental reporting. However, 57.4 per cent of the respondents reported that they would receive better recognition by reporting on environmental issues while 12.4 per cent said that there is no better recognition.

Attitude Towards the Beat

What are the factors that define interest or lack of interest in a journalist towards the beat? About 70 per cent of the total respondents found environmental reporting interesting while 8.6 per cent of the respondents found environmental reporting to be not interesting. Out of the 110 respondents who found environmental reporting interesting, 22.7 per cent of the respondents reported that beat makes him or her feel socially responsible (Table 28). 22 per cent cited the reason that the beat takes him or her closer to man and nature. For 20 per cent of the respondents, environment is related to everyday life and hence reporting on environmental issues is interesting. 18.2 per cent of the respondents related environmental reporting to represent people's cause. For 10.9 per cent of the respondents, the beat gives satisfaction and recognition and for 6.4 per cent of the respondents, the beat is interesting because it is a less explored area and has a lot of scope to find stories. However, the chi-square analysis did not show significant differences among journalists in their perceptions of environmental reporting at P > .05 (X^2=35.24 df=30).

Out of the respondents who said that environmental reporting is not interesting, 28.6 per cent of the respondents reported lack of knowledge on the subject as the reason. 21.6 per cent of the respondents stated that environmental reporting became artificial and self-centered (Table 30). Two respondents from *Mangalam* cited that environmental reporting has no news value and two respondents, one each from *Mangalam* and *Mathrubhumi* reported that there is no glamour attached to environmental reporting. Two other respondents found that there are other issues that are more important. Interestingly, 7.2 per cent of the respondents said that political news items are more sought after by the readers in Kerala newspapers.

Special Qualities

What are the special qualities of a journalist needed to cover environmental issues? For this question, out of the total 162 respondents in the sample, 75.9 per cent reported that they give priority to understanding the issue (Table 31). However, 10.6 per cent thought getting the right information is important, 9.9 per cent said that identifying the right source is important. Two respondents each from the sample found writing the report, on-the-spot study and contacting resource persons as the special qualities needed.

Reliability of the Source

Out of the total 162 respondents in the sample, 69.1 per cent thought that journalists rely on information given by sources while reporting on environmental issues. 19.8 per cent said they can't say whether the sources are reliable or not and 11.1 per cent said that journalists don't rely on information given by sources.

Regarding respondent's perception of the best reliable source to cover environmental issues, 49.4 per cent of the total 162 respondents found citizens as the best reliable source in reporting environmental issues (Table 32). 27.8 per cent of the respondents thought research organizations as the best reliable source and 18.5 per cent of the respondents find environmental agencies as the best reliable source. Four respondents reported government departments as the best reliable source. However two respondents said that self-investigation is important and one respondent said that he would contact resource persons based on the issue.

Regarding the verification of information given by a source, 39.9 per cent of the respondents reported that journalists do their cross-checking with experts in the subject area whereas 27.8 per cent of the respondents say journalists' cross-check with documents available on the issue (Table 33). 7.3 per cent of the respondents say journalists' cross-check with the same source and 2.4 per cent of the respondents say that they do it through journalists from other newspapers. Four respondents said that journalists verify the information with NGOs working on the issue. One respondent said journalists check with other sources and one respondent said they talk to affected people. However 19.7 per cent of the respondents reported that journalists use all the above methods to cross-check the information in hand.

Ethics

When asked whether journalists favour parties involved in the issue while reporting, out of the total 162 respondents in the sample, 37.7 per cent of the respondents said that journalists do favour one party or the other while reporting on environmental issues (Table 35). However, 31.5 per cent of the respondents said that they don't favour and a close 30.8 per cent said that they couldn't say about it.

Out of the total 162 respondents in the sample, 30.2 per cent of the respondents said that journalists suppress news while reporting on environmental issues (Table 36). However, 37.1 per cent of the respondents said that they don't suppress news and 32.7 per cent said that they couldn't say about it.

Out of the 61 respondents who said that journalists do suppress news while reporting on environment, more than half (55.7%) of the respondents said that they do it by supporting a particular side (Table 37). 21.3 per cent of the respondents said that journalists do it by adding a personal outlook to the news item while writing it. 8.2 per cent of the respondents opined that they do it by quoting non-existing sources and another 8.2 per cent said that journalists do it by manipulating their language. Two respondents each cited the methods of either hiding sensitive information or skipping issues of relevance.

About 36.1 per cent of the respondents said that journalists favour business organizations whereas 34.4 per cent reported that the journalists favour victims involved in the issue (Table 38). Six respondents thought that journalists favour the government whereas one respondent thought that journalists favour parties with vested interests in the issue and one respondent felt that journalists stick on to the policy of the newspaper while showing favours in news reports on environment.

Newspaper Coverage of Environmental Issues

News Items

What do journalists think about newspaper readers' preference in news items? For this question, 53.2 per cent respondents reported that readers seek political news stories in newspapers followed by (30.9%) who reported that readers seek human-interest stories and (12.9%) who reported entertainment stories (Table 39). Environment stories had the lowest percentage of 0.6 per cent. No respondent felt that newspaper readers in Kerala seek sensational and crime stories.

Influence

Out of the 162 respondents, a majority of respondents (90.1%) said that society learns much about environment through newspapers. However, 2.5 per cent reported that they couldn't say about it. And out of the respondents who felt that society learns much about environment through newspapers, 98.6 per cent said that environmental reports in the newspapers do influence the society. A minority of 0.7 per cent opined that they don't influence the society and another 0.7 per cent couldn't say about it.

Asked about who is influenced most, a majority of 87.5 per cent respondents said that readers would be influenced through environmental news reports. 7.6 per cent said that government would be influenced most (Table 40). 2.8 per cent of the respondents opined that NGOs could be influenced closely followed by 2.1 per cent respondents who said that politicians would be influenced.

Quality of Reporting

Respondents were asked to measure quality of environmental reporting in Kerala newspapers on a four-point scale viz. very good, good, bad and very bad. A closely half (54.3%) of the respondents rated that quality of environmental reporting was good although 38.3 per cent of the respondents said that environmental coverage was poor (Table 41). However, 4.3 per cent of the respondents reported that quality of environmental reporting was very poor and 3.1 per cent said that quality of reporting was very good.

Training

Asked whether training is needed for journalists to cover environmental issues better, a majority of 96.2 per cent said that better training was required for journalists in covering environmental issues. Regarding the type of training 52.4 per cent preferred to have special courses on environment (Table 45). 23.2 per cent each preferred periodic training and expert's lectures. However 1.2 per cent said that self-study could lead to better understanding of the issue.

Role of Newspaper Management

To the question can newspaper management play a key role in promoting coverage of environment, 83.3 per cent thought it could play a key role. About 7 per cent said that management could not play any role and 9.9 per cent said that they couldn't say about it.

Among the 135 respondents who opined that newspaper management plays a key role in promoting coverage of environment, 29.6 per cent of the respondents said that management should give more space for environmental news (Table 46). 20.8 per cent said that it could be through better environment friendly editorial policies. 14.8 per cent of the respondents reported that better training should be given to the journalists by the management to report on environmental issues. Another 14.8 per cent suggested setting up team of environmental journalists in each bureau whereas 12.6 per cent of the respondents needed moral support and 7.4 per cent needed more freedom in coverage.

Perceptions of Journalists

Risk

Out of the total 162 respondents in the sample, 81.4 per cent of the respondents have reported that journalists do face risks when they report on environment. However, 9.3 per cent of the respondents have viewed that they don't face any kind of risk, yet 9.3 per cent felt that they can't say about it. As regards the kind of risk faced by journalists while reporting environmental issues, 34.6 per cent of the respondents reported that they face legal problems whereas 31.2 per cent of the respondents said that they face physical violence and 30.7 per cent of the respondents said they faced harassment and 3.5 per cent of the respondent said they feared loss of employment (Table 47).

Journalist's Support to the Environment

42.5 per cent of the respondents were of the opinion that they can support environment by creating awareness among readers through wider coverage whereas 28.5 per cent of the respondents felt that journalists should undertake investigative studies on environmental issues, and 22.2 per cent feel that they should report more environmental stories and try to give prominence (Table 48). 5.6 per cent respondents felt that journalists should take up special themes on environment on a regular basis.

Commitment

Out of the 138 respondents who said that journalist's commitment to environment can improve reporting, 22.5 per cent of the respondents said that journalists should study the issues better (Table 57). This is closely followed by 21.7 per cent of the respondents who said better commitment could develop interest to undertake and publish investigative studies. 17.4 per cent of the respondents thought that environment is a social responsibility and needs commitment on part of the journalists whereas 16.7 per cent of the respondents thought that commitment could lead to better involvement with the issues. However, 15.2 per cent of the respondents felt that filing stories in the right perspective could show his or her commitment while 5.1 per cent of the respondents said that they could convince the management in reporting an issue.

Role of Newspapers in Environmental Issues

Out of the 162 respondents a majority of 92.6 per cent respondents thought that newspapers could campaign on various environmental issues simultaneously. In this context, 83.3 per cent reported that there is an increased awareness on environmental issues among the people through coverage of newspapers in Kerala. However 10.4 per cent of the respondents felt that newspapers have not increased awareness and 12.3 per cent of the respondents said that they couldn't say about it.

Incentives

Can better incentives for journalists improve environmental reporting? To this specific question, 44 per cent of the respondents thought that special incentives from the government could encourage environmental reporting. However 41.4 per cent reported that special incentives would not make any difference and 14.2 per cent of the respondents could not say anything to this question. Out of the 72 respondents who described that special incentives from the government could encourage environmental reporting, 40.3 per cent preferred free training on environmental reporting (Table 61). 36.1 per cent viewed special cash awards as the best incentive and 23.6 per cent reported free transport facilities could encourage environmental reporting.

Role of Media in Environmental Education

Should newspapers join hands with such agencies in educating people on environment? For this question, out of the 162 respondents in the sample, majority of 90.1 per cent reported that newspapers could support initiatives on environmental education. However, 3.7 per cent said that newspapers could not support such initiatives and 6.2 per cent answered can't say.

Content Analysis

In order to ascertain coverage given to environmental issues *vis-à-vis* other news items, content analysis technique has been used. A total of 350 newspaper editions of seven dailies covering four cities viz., Thiruvananthapuram, Kottayam, Kochi and Kozhikode have been analyzed for the purpose. In the analysis, it was found that *Mangalam* (3.7%) followed by *Deshabhimani* (3%) allocated more percentage of news items to environment as compared to other newspapers. However, all the newspapers did not allocate more than four per cent of news items to environment (Table 64).

However, in the analysis of different environmental issues, *Malayala Manorama* (48) and *Deshabhimani* (48) gave equal number of items followed by *The Hindu* (46) and *Mangalam* (46) in terms of frequency of news items. However *Kerala Kaumudi* (22) allocated less frequency of items as compared to other news items. In the break-up of coverage given to different news items, solid/hazardous waste disposal got more coverage in all seven newspapers in comparison to other news items (Table 65).

In terms of coverage in each city, Kozhikode (96) obtained more coverage of environmental issues followed by Kochi (84), Kottayam (52) and Thiruvananthapuram (50). Further, in terms of coverage given to different environmental issues, solid/ hazardous waste got more coverage in Kozhikode whereas river pollution got more coverage in Kochi (Table 66). However, in Kottayam two categories of news items, agriculture and drinking water pollution did not get any coverage while drinking water pollution was not given any coverage in Thiruvananthapuram (Table 66).

Conclusions

Research scholars have found that the mass media act as both an important motivator and indicator of public concerns. Indeed, the media have been not only disseminating information between policy-makers and the public but also shaping public perception and opinion. In relation to environmental issues, the media raise the level of environmental awareness while focusing the attention of citizens on specific environmental issues. For instance, a senior journalist observed, "Newspapers have played a great role in maintaining this high level of awareness. Today's generation is better aware of environment especially in the case of issues like urban waste including plastic." (Case Study 2)

In general, newspapers have been found to be one of the most predominant sources of environmental information available to the public, particularly in developing countries. The print media, especially daily newspapers, offer environmental coverage through reportage, editorial commentary, as well as documentation of environmental events and issues. The media serve an educational and political role in directing the popular discussion about environmental issues. Since environment is vital for leading a good quality of life, journalists who act as mass educators in influencing the people, bureaucrats, policy-makers and politicians play a crucial role. In the study, it was found that 66.7 per cent of the respondents believed that the newspapers in Kerala report environmental issues frequently. But, about 31 per cent of the respondents disagreed with the view. In fact, the perceptions of journalists were verified by content-analyzing all these seven newspapers that figured in the sample. It was found that the frequency of reporting was less than four per cent, and all the newspapers did report occasionally although environmental issues were expected to occupy much space in the newspapers. Further, those reports that appeared in the newspapers were event-centered instead of newspaper initiatives as 68.5 per cent of the respondents in the study responded that environmental news appear when an issue surfaces. Because most of the issues are reported when an NGO, or the government takes the initiative. For example, when the *chikunguniya* (fever) was rampant, the people were of the view that the hazardous solid waste deposits in the city limits were the cause. As people started disposing it of, newspapers reported the issue because of the people's initiatives.

Moreover, Kerala newspapers too report environmental stories when there is a conflict of interest between two parties. Therefore, 29 per cent of the respondents felt that conflict has a greater news value in the coverage of environmental issues. This view has been substantiated in the content analysis of newspapers. Newspapers focused on the coverage of court proceedings related to environment because of conflict between two parties.

Further, nearly 49 per cent of the respondents cited man's indifference as the reason for environmental issues. Truly, most of the environmental problems in Kerala related to man's ignorance and lackadaisical attitude. For example, waste disposal, particularly hazardous solid waste from hospitals was increasingly becoming a problem. Adding to it, digging of river beds for sand to be used for house construction is also becoming another environmental problem in the state. In spite of government measures to contain the practice, it is not successful.

Therefore, to a specific question, whether newspapers do require an environmental reporter, about 92 per cent of the respondents felt that newspapers in Kerala require a journalist on the environmental beat. Most of the newspapers in Kerala don't have an exclusive journalist to cover the environment, and general reporters are assigned the task to cover the issue whenever an environmental crisis erupts because environment is seen as an event-centered issue, instead of a long process to be covered. Thus, it is seen in the study that only 9.3 per cent of the reporters covered environment very frequently. Although journalists expressed the view that they wanted to report on environment, they were not assigned the work. Further, 81.5 per cent of the respondents reported satisfaction while reporting environmental issues. As seen in the study 70 per cent of the print journalists found environmental reporting as interesting. Thus, more than half of them expressed the view that there is a lack of opportunity to report and some others (21.2%) did not have time to report environment.

In the study, it was found that 76 per cent reported that they give utmost importance to study the issue in detail in response to the question that journalists do require special qualities to cover environment. Therefore, 67 per cent of the respondents rely on the information given by sources. In the coverage of issues related to pollution, chemical waste and others, the respondents replied that the government and NGOs were the reliable source. Mostly, environmental issues were reported basing on a single source, instead of multiple sources. Although environmental issues are expected to be covered by collecting information from multiple sources, the single source stories have been found predominantly in all the newspapers. Further, investigative stories have not been found in the analysis of news reports.

Further, with regard to the news coverage, 53 per cent of respondents reported that newspaper readers seek political news stories. Haque (1986) observed:

> Politics is the most newsworthy topic in India. The drama of conflict among different parties within the political process and within the parties themselves has been suggested to have an enormous fascination for the middle class readers who constitute the majority of the newspaper readers.

Truly, Indian newspapers give much coverage to political news, and Kerala being the first state in the country with cent per cent literacy is no exception. Therefore, environmental issues get less priority although the respondents said that 87.5 per cent of readers would be influenced through environmental news reports. As regards the quality of reporting, 54 per cent reported that quality of reporting was good although 38.3 per cent reported that environmental reporting was poor. In fact, the content analysis revealed that most of the reports appeared like news reports by quoting government officials or one source story like press conferences. Most of the reports adopted a summary lead instead of giving a human interest angle as the study found that 13 per cent of the respondents seek human interest stories but none of the news reports in the analysis used human interest lead.

In relation to legal knowledge, about 75 per cent of the respondents agreed that journalists face legal problems in the coverage of environmental issues. The content analysis of newspapers showed majority of environmental reports dealt with court proceedings. Unless reporters have legal knowledge they increasingly face a problem from the judiciary. Apart from it, for the wrong coverage of environmental issues, newspapers are prone to legal controversies. Therefore 81 per cent of the respondents agreed that they face a risk, out of which 34.6 per cent of the respondents perceived that they face risk in the form of legal problems. Most of the environmental issues are embroiled in legal issues; and hence a few reporters show interest in the coverage of these issues. However, 31 per cent of the respondents opined that they face physical violence if they cover environmental issues. For instance, case study 7 shows that "money is an important factor in tackling the environmental issues. There is threat for the life of the reporter who goes for reporting issues like sand mining where large amount of money is at stake by the mafia".

Overall, the study finds that the journalists have the following perceptions:

1. More than half of the respondents believed that

environmental issues appear when an environmental issue surfaces.

2. Majority of the respondents perceived that man's indifference was the main reason for environmental destruction.
3. More than 90 per cent of the respondents expressed the view that there should be an environmental reporter in all newspapers.
4. Nearly half of the respondents informed that citizens are the best reliable source on reporting environmental issues.
5. Nearly one-third of the respondents viewed that journalists suppress news while reporting environmental issues out of which more than half said that they do it by supporting a particular party.
6. More than half of the respondents perceived that readers seek political news followed by human interest stories.
7. Respondents perceived that risk is involved in the coverage of environmental issues.
8. More than 90 per cent of the respondents said that newspapers could campaign on environmental issues.
9. About 44 per cent of the respondents said that special incentives from the government can encourage better coverage of environmental issues.
10. More than 95 per cent of the respondents said that journalists require better training in covering environmental issues.

In view of the random sampling method adopted for the study, the results can be generalized to the universe of the study for survey and content analysis. In the study, 68.5 per cent of the respondents responded that environmental news appears when an issue surfaces. In this regard, the present study agrees with the earlier studies done in different settings in relation to coverage of environment (Anderson, 1997; Molotch and Lester, 1974, Rubin and Sachs, 1973, Sachsman, 1976, Wilkins and Patterson, 1987). These studies pointed out that the coverage of environmental issues are event-centered and the present study too found that the environmental issues are covered when there is a dramatic event.

The study also found that the respondents depend on government and industry sources. In this respect, the present study is similar to the earlier studies (Taylor *et al.*, 2000; Sigal, 1986; Brown *et al.*, 1987) that the reporters rely on government and official sources. Interestingly, the present study found that about 49 per cent of the respondents expressed that citizens were the best reliable source particularly in the coverage of issues related to sand mining and drying of the rivers. This finding differs from the earlier studies as none of the earlier studies found that the citizens were the source of information. For example, sand mining at the river beds is undertaken clandestinely without the knowledge of the government officials in Kerala. Hence, the respondents expressed the view that in such issues, the local people are the best source of information.

The coverage of environmental issues is very less in Kerala newspapers. In this respect too, the present study is close to the earlier studies (Vilanialam, 1993; Prita and Karippai, 1996) because the definition of environmental news in all the studies is found to be similar.

The present study has found that newspapers do not have a particular reporter to cover environmental issues in Kerala including the national dailies such as *The Hindu* and *The New Indian Express*. Therefore it is suggested that newspapers can assign one reporter to cover environmental issues exclusively. The study also found out that more than 95 per cent of the respondents expressed the view that a systematic training should be given to cover environmental issues. It is seen in the study that most of respondents have high academic qualification [post-graduates (80.9%) and Ph.D. holders (1.2%)] and hence newspapers can depute them for further training periodically to study environmental issues. Because environment coverage cannot be event centered and it is a long process, training will enrich the journalists' knowledge, thereby quality of environmental reporting can be improved.

The study also found out that environmental reporting is interesting for majority of journalists. Such training may sustain their interest in environmental reporting. Further, the study found that most of the journalists do not have legal knowledge. It is advisable that journalists can be trained in environmental law as the central and state governments are enacting new laws related to environment. In addition, 44 per cent of the respondents thought that incentives from the government would encourage environmental reporting. Therefore it is suggested that the Kerala Government may encourage environmental reporting by instituting a prize or a cash in recognition of the service rendered to the society. The study also found that 6.4 per cent of the respondents expressed the view that the environmental reporting gives them recognition. This perception may be acceptable in the context of environmental reporting.

As found out in the study, the newspapers give low coverage to environmental issues. It is suggested that newspapers can increase the frequency of coverage of environmental issues and create awareness among people. The study found that more than one-fourth of the respondents (29.6%) also felt that the management can give more space for environmental issues while 20.8 per cent of them said that environment friendly editorial policies will help the coverage of the environmental issues. Specifically, 42.5 per cent of the respondents are of the opinion that they can support environment by creating awareness among readers. Because Kerala is the first state in the country to have achieved cent per cent literacy, political awareness is found to be higher as compared to other states in the country. Therefore, in this regard the newspaper management can also play a crucial role in raising the awareness of the people in relation to environmental issues. In creating environmental awareness, newspapers can continuously campaign on specific environmental issues or projects. For instance, solid waste disposal, pesticides and river pollution need special attention from newspapers in creating awareness among the people. Therefore in this regard, the study found that 90 per cent of the respondents felt that newspapers can support initiatives on environmental education. Since mass media are considered a public educator, their role in this regard is increasingly needed.

APPENDIX–I

Environmental Movements in India

The environmental movement in India, which began in 1972, the year of Stockholm Conference, spread over several voluntary organizations and non-governmental organizations. They have an impressive record of confrontation and cooperation in promoting environmental education, creating environmental awareness among people by interaction and consultation with government officials and people from all walks of life, such as consumers, contractors, industrialists, multinational companies, engineers and academicians. The knowledge, technical skill, judgment and orientation regarding the environment have been, and is continuing to be significant. They have also contributed considerably in mobilizing public opinion for the promotion of environment in some trouble-spots of the country.

The non-governmental organizations in India are involved in several types of activities such as environmental education and awareness, natural resources conservation, pollution control, afforestation, and social forestry, rural development, wildlife conservation, waste utilization, family welfare and population control and eco-development.

The role of ecological considerations in social movements is certainly ambiguous and ambitious. In India, those who constitute the movement are engaged in a livelihood struggle and that this livelihood struggle can be successful only if the environment is managed in a sustainable way. The concerns of these movements with the distribution of resources are usually linked to the idea about the alternative uses to which they could be put.

The Chipko Movement

Since the last century, the state has continually encroached upon the rights and privileges of the people to forest resources. The resistance to this encroachment has taken traditional Gandhian form, in the power of Satyagraha or peaceful non-cooperation. Swami Chidanandji, a spiritual leader, who had travelled widely all over the world and had seen the ecological crisis in the so called developed world, took the message of the Stockholm Conference to the hill villages in September-October 1972.

Prompted by his message, people in the forest areas of Gharwal Himalaya, revived the type of protest, which had originally been directed at the British, and used against the state of Uttar Pradesh. Confrontation with the state came when several ash trees were allotted to a sports goods company of Allahabad in the Mandal forest. When a single tree was refused on silvicultural grounds to the villagers for making yokes, people questioned this decision and declared their determination to save trees by hugging. This was repeated in other valleys and thus a non-violent technique of resistance emerged.

The word 'Chipko' means hugging the trees, and was popularized through the folk songs of Chipko activist Ghanshyam Sailani. In its revived form, the civil disobedience practiced by Chipko adherents has taken on an increasingly ecological character. "Although it had its roots in a movement based on politics of the distribution of the benefits of resources, it soon became an ecological movement rooted in politics of distribution of ecological costs" (Bandyopadhyay and Shiva, 1989).

Chipko is post-independent India's most powerful ecological movement. Chipko's first battle took place in April

24, 1973 in Chamoli district when villagers of Mandal, led by Chandi Prasad Bhatt and Dasholi Gram Swarajya Mandal (DGSM), prevented the Allahabad based sports goods company 'Symonds' from felling ash trees. In December, the villagers stopped Symond's agents from tree felling in the Phata-Rampur forest about 60 km. from Gopeshwar. Another turning point for Chipko was that for the first time women took active part in it (Mitra, 2001).

In Tehri Garhwal, Chipko activists led by Sunderlal Bahuguna began organizing villagers to oppose tree-felling in the Henwal valley in 1977. They resorted to direct action in December 1977 to protect forests. The following year, many volunteers, including women, were arrested for opposing a forest auction at Narendranagar. The struggle in Henwal marked the transformation of Chipko from an economic struggle to a fight for conservation (Mitra, 2001). Chandi Prasad Bhatt coordinated its early protests and then involved village women with great success in the reclamation and afforestation of the degraded land. Bahuguna organized important Chipko protests in Tehri Garhwal between 1976 and 1980. The third Chipko faction is the Uttarakhand Sangharsh Vahini. It provided a radical focus to the movement in the late 1970s, but its dedicated core of student activists has since gone their individual ways (Guha, 1991).

Behind Chipko lies a century of peasant protests against commercial foresty in the Himalaya. It was Chandi Prasad Bhatt who formed the DGSM in 1964 in Gopeshwar. A Sarvodaya movement offshoot, it worked to promote Vinoba Bhave's concepts of 'sramadan' and a non-violent, self-reliant society comprising villages based on rural industries. At both national and global levels, Chipko helped consolidate in the first stages, awareness that deforestation, soil erosion and floods are linked to the fragility of mountain ecosystems. Chipko was also interpreted as a critique of the overall development process and as an assertion of the rights of the villagers whose labour and resources are subordinated to the demands of the industrial sector (Guha, 1991).

Chipko movement emphasizes on two themes: (1) ecology is permanent economy (2) the most important forest products are not timber, but soil, water and air. Further, in Uttarakhand, the Chipko movement has gone one step further from protecting and planting trees to challenging mining and dam building. Today Chipko Movement is looked at by many people as the first true ecological movement of the people. Undoubtedly it has the following successes:

- It has slowed down, if not totally stopped, the process of deforestation in the Uttarakhand.
- It has exposed the vested interests involved in the mass-destruction of forests.
- It has given the people of the region a rallying point to collectively oppose the exploitation of their natural resources.
- It has created awareness among the people regarding the implications of ecological destruction.
- It has demonstrated the workability of a powerful model of people's participation, a model that can be emulated and replicated (Khanna and Nath, 1990).

Silent Valley Movement

The Silent Valley movement stands out as one of the most important milestones in the shaping of public opinion as well as the formulation of official policy. The Silent Valley hydroelectric project in Kerala is the only scheme, which has been halted on environmental grounds. Hydroelectric power generation unlike thermal and nuclear is clean and uses a renewable natural resource. The Silent Valley hydroelectric project which would have dammed the Kunti river in Palghat district was seen as a perfect site from engineering and hydrological point of view. The power produced could have helped to start industries and create employment in Kerala. It is difficult to convince anyone that a dam, by creating a reservoir and in the process flooding a forest tract may be causing ecological damage.

The people of Kerala felt that the construction of the dam and hydro-electric power station in Silent Valley should be shelved. And pursued under umbrella organizations like Kerala Sastra Sahitya Parishad, the Society for the Protection of the Silent Valley and 'Da Vinci' environmentalists. The people petitioned the government to educate the common people and fought hard to get a proper assessment of the project done.

Although the British identified Silent Valley as an ideal site for the generation of hydel power as early as in 1929, technical investigations were carried out in 1958. The Planning Commission sanctioned the project in 1973. In 1977, a report known as the Futhehally report titled "Report of the task force for the Ecological Planning of the Western Ghats" referred to what was envisaged in Silent Valley (Futehally, 1977). The report pointed out that the project cost would probably have to be revised and how capital losses like the forests, which would be submerged, had not been taken into account. The disturbance to the forest, by humans who would come to construct the dam, was also cited. The report said "the result will be that the last vestige of natural climate vegetation of the region and one of the last remaining in the country will be lost to posterity and various adverse ecological consequences will follow. The task force feels very strongly that the project should be shelved and the area declared a biosphere reserve. It seems unjustifiable to sacrifice this unique environment for the sake of generating 120MW of power (Futehally, 1977).

"Save the Silent Valley" day was observed throughout the state. B.G. Verghese, a noted journalist wrote articles to create public awareness. Public meetings were held. The Gandhi Peace Foundation joined the campaign. Academics, scientists, environmentalists and public-spirited men throughout the country to serve as a focal point of public action against the project formed organizations. An attempt was made by the 'Friends of Trees' and the 'Society for the Protection of Silent Valley' at the High Court of Kerala to halt the execution of the project. A stay order was obtained from the court and this gave a temporary respite. Nevertheless people outside the state of Kerala who were concerned about the issue formed the second group. They were vocal through organizations like the Bombay Natural History Society and the Save the Silent Valley Committee.

The third group was of the scientists and experts, who were agitating over the project and offered their expertise and views, and served in various governmental and non-governmental committees. Points and counterpoints were made, pamphlets and books were published and counter allegations made. However, one remarkable result of this was that every possible aspect of the issue was examined in the greatest possible detail and scientific debates were made public. The movement offered a unique foresight of people's participation, calling for right to information as an integral part of right to liberty.

APPENDIX–II

Environmental Issues in Kerala

The major environmental issues in Kerala are listed below. The data pertaining to these environmental issues have been collected from various sources such as internet, magazines, books, newspapers and so on.

Industrial Pollution

Rivers of Kerala have been increasingly polluted from the industrial and domestic waste, from the pesticides and fertilizer used in agriculture. Major rivers like Periyar and Chaliyar are polluted by hazardous pollutants like phosphates, sulphides, ammonia, fluorides, heavy metals and insecticides. It is estimated that nearly 260 million litres of industrial effluents reach the Periyar river daily from the Kochi industrial belt. The industrial belt of Eloor near Kochi is one of the world's 'top toxic hot spots' according to international environment group, Greenpeace (Anonymous, 2008a). Another major water quality problem associated with rivers of Kerala is bacteriological pollution. With regard to groundwater, water quality characteristics of wells in Kerala are found to be affected by chemical and biological contaminants mainly because of the presence of excess chloride. Open wells of Kerala are under the threat of bacteriological contamination.

Drying up of Rivers

Even though Kerala gets six months of rainfall, 2.5 times higher than the national average, the state experiences water scarcity with conditions worsening in some regions. For example river Nila, which is a perennial river, is reduced to a trickle much of the time. Even though the peculiar slanting topography of the state and the high density of population are highlighted as the main factors for the acute drinking water crisis in the state, it's mismanagement of biodiversity including water resources that has led to the present water crisis in the state (Venugopal, 2006). Besides the natural factors, human induced problems by way of faulty, unscientific land use practices, paddy wetland reclamations, deforestation, sand mining, urbanisation etc. have affected water sources of the state. Because of the severe habitat destruction, much of the highland area has been deforested. Rivers that were perennial until a few years ago turn into beds of sand during the lean months, and wells dry up before the summer peaks; many villages and towns depending on tanker lorries peddling water. With the increase in residential construction, illegal sand mining has decimated riverbeds. The removal of sand has resulted in a faster flow to the sea and less renewal of the water table. The inland waterways from Trivandrum to Kochi and beyond are turning into stinking, stagnant water bodies.

Hazardous Solid Waste Disposal

The generation of municipal solid waste, industrial hazardous waste, biomedical waste and agricultural waste has been rapidly increasing due to population growth, lifestyle changes, economic development, changes in agricultural activities and changed consumerism. However the waste management techniques have not kept pace with the increasing quantity of solid waste (Gopikrishna and Sasi Kumar, 2006). Solid waste generated from household garbage, waste from shops, markets, hotels, slaughterhouses and poultry farms are piled up frequently due to lack of a proper solid waste management system. Untreated biodegradable solid wastes have created the fear of pathogenic and numerous diseases causing microorganisms. Indiscriminate disposal of metallic and plastic articles are choking the drains and rivulets, which can result in unexpected floods.

Use of Pesticides

Rampant use of pesticides has given rise to several short-term and long-term adverse effects of the chemicals. The first report of poisoning due to pesticides was reported from Kerala in 1958 whereover 100 people died after consuming wheat flour contaminated with pesticides (Indiradevi, 2007). Rice cultivation in Kuttanad is more intensive than in many other parts of the state. Nearly 90% of the farmers sow high-yielding varieties and this means they have to use high levels of chemical inputs. Skin problems are the most common problem linked to pesticide use in Kuttanad area of the state. Itching, eye-irritation and vision problems are also very common. Symptoms also include breathing problems, dehydration, vomiting, cramps and diarrhea. There has been widespread contamination of food commodities with pesticide residues, basically due to non-judicious use of pesticides and has led to immune-suppression, hormone disruption, diminished intelligence, reproductive abnormalities, and cancer. Nearly 135 people have lost their lives because of the aerial spraying of the highly hazardous endosulfan by the government-owned Plantation Corporation of Kerala in an area of nearly 4,700 acres in Kasaragod.

Chemical Waste

Indiscriminate use of chemical fertilizers in Kerala is polluting land; pesticides poison water and air, and leave their residue on foodstuff. Even the fauna has been badly affected by the over-use of chemicals. The demand for pesticides and fertilizers, the vital constituents of modern agriculture practices, has increased recently due to the need to protect high yielding crops. A recent study by Kerala's groundwater department has traced toxic chemicals in the groundwater at a multinational plant in Pudussery panchayat in the arid Palakkad district. Water samples from the factory site was found to have presence of calcium, magnesium, chloride and sodium in them (Anonymous, 2008b). A Greenpeace study had established that most of the fertilizer, insecticide and chemical manufacturing plants in the Eloor-Edayar region dumping toxic waste into the Periyar river resulting in the incidence of diseases, respiratory, dermatological and even psychological.

Destruction of Paddy Fields

Cost escalation of rice production and the rise in the demand for house plots have led to the 'land-filling' of several acres of paddy fields all over the state. The near total elimination of rice culture in Kerala is sure to create huge ecological calamities like deluge, depletion of groundwater wealth and drinking water scarcity (Hali, 2006). It will also shrink the garden land cultivation, homestead farming, backyard poultry, cattle rearing, dairy farming and several avocations. Rice culture is slowly paving way to large scale reclamation and all transactions in the rice area take place between real estate personnel and construction firms. It is also resulting in the levelling of hills and hillocks leading to ecological disorders. Drinking water has become a scarce commodity in several areas and households are buying it daily from suppliers. Further, removal of soil from the bushy hilly terrains for filling the low-lying areas such as paddy fields and marshlands for construction activities has also led to the declining of the natural rainwater conservation.

Pollution of Rivers and Backwaters

Effluents from the various factories have polluted the sea, rivers and backwaters throughout the state. Unabated reclamation, silting and pollution from industries and human wastes are damaging the estuarine and backwater ecosystem. A report prepared by the Kerala State Council for Science Technology and Environment (KSCSTE) says that the rivers in the State are being increasingly polluted from the industrial and domestic waste, pesticides and fertilizers used in agriculture. The State Environment Report, Kerala, 2005, published by the Council also pointed out that Periyar and Chaliyaar rivers were examples of pollution of water bodies due to industrial effluents (Anonymous, 2008c). Faecal contamination is affecting 90 per cent of the wells in the State.

The report cited that coastal environment degradation of wetlands, mangroves, mud-banks, beaches, estuaries and cliffs, which are important habitats of marine and coastal environment, are in various stages of degradation. Unabated reclamation, silting and pollution from industries and human wastes are damaging the estuarine and backwater ecosystem, the report said.

Destruction of Hills

Large-scale destruction of hills in various pockets of the state mainly to fill the paddy fields and for construction activities has resulted in environmental disasters and water scarcity. Further, several hills are being crushed down, destroying the topographical features of the area. Rock mines and metal crushes are creating problems like heavy metal leaching and their accumulation leading to health hazards like silicosis, cadmium and mercury poisoning to the nearby inhabitants (Sinilal, 2007). Bricks made from clay and mined from paddy fields have led to the loss of fertile soil enriched with organic matter. Clay mining has given rise to water displacement of the trenches. Gravel mining from river beds is also going on in an uncontrolled level bringing down the groundwater level which in turn brings about shortage of water.

Deforestation

Forests covered 65 per cent of Kerala in 1905. However, according to Economic Review, 2004, the state's forests account only for 29 per cent of its area (Venugopal, 2006). Disappearance of forests has led to vanishing forest cover for the watershed of the rivers. Several hydroelectric projects have also resulted in the denuding of vast stretches of forestland. According to a study conducted by National Remote Sensing Agency in 1980, forests had been reduced to nine per cent (Venugopal, 2006). Deforestation has also resulted in soil erosion, which has quickened the runoff, reducing the percolation of water and thus the replenishment of groundwater. Even afforestation attempts by the government have affected the groundwater situation adversely as the majority of trees planted are acacia and eucalyptus both of which have deep roots and suck out the groundwater.

Sand Mining

There is a sharp fall in the underground water table in the river basins in Kerala after the rains, as a result of deforestation and indiscriminate sand mining resulting in the deepening of riverbeds. Sand mining, coupled with destruction of forests in the state, have adversely affected the river system (Nair, 2005). The underground water table in the catchment areas and the river basins is related to the surface water level in rivers. Indiscriminate sand mining during the past two decades has deepened the riverbeds by an average three to four metres, while there are points where it has dropped by six metres. Consequently, the water table in the wells in the catchment areas and the river basins has also fallen sharply to the surface water levels in the rivers. Another significant factor contributing negatively to rainwater conservation is the removal of soil from the bushy hilly terrains for filling low-lying areas such as paddy fields and marshlands for construction activities. If these activities are not controlled and regulated by the authorities, the water scarcity in the state will become serious in the years to come, albeit it is already acute in the mid and high lands in several districts.

APPENDIX–III

Questionnaire

Environment and Newspapers: Perceptions of Print Journalists in Kerala

I. Identification data Code No.

1. Age:
2. Gender: Male/Female
3. Education level:
   (a) Under Graduate
   (b) Graduate
   (c) Postgraduate
   (d) Any other.....................................
4. Income per annum:
5. Native place:
6. If you are not a native of Kerala, please state the reason for working in Kerala?

   ....

7. Mother tongue:
8. Designation:
9. How long have you been working as a journalist:
10. Name of the paper in which you are working at present:

11. Are you satisfied with the present job?
    (*a*) Yes
    (*b*) No
    (*c*) Can't say

12. If Yes or No, how do you describe your satisfaction?
    (*a*) Very Good
    (*b*) Good
    (*c*) Bad
    (*d*) Very Bad

13. If Very Good or Good, please explain the reason for your satisfaction?
    (*a*) Good working environment
    (*b*) Comfortable salary
    (*c*) Job security
    (*d*) Any other....................................

14. If Bad or Very Bad, please explain the reason?
    (*a*) Low salary
    (*b*) Lack of support of management
    (*c*) Lack of other opportunities
    (*d*) Any other....................................

II. Professional Obligations

15. Do you think that the profession of journalism can help the society?
    (*a*) Yes
    (*b*) No
    (*c*) Can't say

16. If yes, in what way can the profession help the society? (Please rank your response)

    S.No. *Reason* *Rank*

    (*a*) It can create awareness among readers
    (*b*) It can make the government's act
    (*c*) It can support people's cause
    (*d*) Any other.....................

17. If no, can you tell me the reason?
    (Please rank your response)

S.No.	*Reason*	*Rank*
(a)	It doesn't create awareness among readers	
(b)	It cannot make the government's act	
(c)	It cannot support people's cause	
(d)	Any other....................................	

18. Do you think newspapers in Kerala report environmental issues frequently?
    (a) Yes
    (b) No
    (c) Can't say

19. When do you think more environmental issues appear in Kerala newspapers?
    (a) When an environmental issue surfaces
    (b) When there is an environmental conflict
    (c) Any other....................................

20. What do you think is the main reason for environmental problems in Kerala? (Please rank your response)

S.No.	*Reason*	*Rank*
(a)	Industrialization	
(b)	Man's indifference to environment	
(c)	Lack of proper legal structure	
(d)	Lack of interest by government	
(e)	Lack of proper planning	
(f)	Any other....................................	

21. During your career as a journalist, have you reported on environmental issues?
    (a) Yes
    (b) No
    (c) Can't say

22. If yes, how frequently have you reported on environment?

(*a*) Very frequently
(*b*) Frequently
(*c*) Less frequently

23. Please list out few environmental issues you have reported during your career?

24. If so, how many environmental issues did you report during 2004-05 and 2005-06? (Give approximate figures)
(*a*) 2004-05 : ______________
(*b*) 2005-06 :______________

25. If no, can you tell me the reason? (Please rank your response)

S.No.	*Reason*	*Rank*
(*a*)	Lack of opportunity to report	
(*b*)	Unable to report though opportunity is there	
(*c*)	Lack of encouragement from superiors	
(*d*)	Lack of time to pursue the issues	
(*e*)	Any other....................................	

26. Do you think reporting on environmental issues can get you satisfaction?
(*a*) Yes
(*b*) No
(*c*) Can't say

27. If you report on environmental issues, do you think that you will receive recognition among your colleagues/peers/journalists?
(*a*) Yes
(*b*) No
(*c*) Can't say

28. Do you think that newspapers in Kerala require a journalist to be on environmental beat?
(*a*) Yes
(*b*) No
(*c*) Can't say

29. Do you think environmental reporting is interesting for journalists?
    (a) Yes
    (b) No
    (c) Can't say

30. If yes, please tell us the reason?________________

31. If no, please tell us the reason?________________

32. Do you think environmental reporting is difficult for journalists to cover?
    (a) Yes
    (b) No
    (c) Can't say

33. If so, in covering an environmental issue, do you think journalist requires special qualities? (Please rank your response)

S.No.	*Qualities*	*Rank*
(a)	Understanding the issue	
(b)	Getting the right information	
(c)	Identifying the right sources	
(d)	Writing the report	
(e)	Any other....................................	

34. Do you think journalists rely on information given by sources to cover environmental issues?
    (a) Yes
    (b) No
    (c) Can't say

35. Which do you think is the best reliable source among the following? (Please rank your response)

S.No.	*Source*	*Rank*
(a)	Government Department	
(b)	Citizens	
(c)	Environmental agencies	
(d)	Research organizations	

(*e*) Industry
(*f*) Any other......................................

36. How do you verify the information given by a source?
(*a*) By cross-checking the information from the same source
(*b*) Through journalists working in the other newspapers
(*c*) Through checking documents available on the issue
(*d*) By cross-checking with experts
(*e*) By verifying it with NGOs
(*f*) All the above
(*g*) Any other......................................

37. Do you think that journalists reporting on environmental issues favour some parties involved in the issue?
(*a*) Yes
(*b*) No
(*c*) Can't say

38. Do you think journalists suppress news while reporting on environment?
(*a*) Yes
(*b*) No
(*c*) Can't say

39. If yes, how do you think they suppress news?
(*a*) By quoting non-existing sources
(*b*) By manipulating the language
(*c*) By supporting a particular side
(*d*) By including a personal outlook
(*e*) Any other......................................

40. If yes, whom do you think they mostly favour?
(*a*) Government
(*b*) Business organizations
(*c*) Victims involved in the issue
(*d*) Environmentalists
(*e*) Any other......................................

41. In reporting on environmental issues, do you think journalists are answerable?
    (*a*) Yes
    (*b*) No
    (*c*) Can't say

42. If yes, to whom will the journalist be answerable? (Please rank your response)

    S.No. To whom *Rank*

    (*a*) Readers
    (*b*) Newspaper management
    (*c*) Government
    (*d*) Research organizations
    (*e*) Environmental NGOs
    (*f*) Any other.....................................

43. While covering environmental issues, do you think journalists face legal problems?
    (*a*) Yes
    (*b*) No
    (*c*) Can't say

44. If so, do you think journalists' require special legal knowledge?
    (*a*) Yes
    (*b*) No
    (*c*) Can't say

45. Do you think journalists face risk from the parties involved?
    (*a*) Yes
    (*b*) No
    (*c*) Can't say

46. If yes, can you describe the type of risk?
    (*a*) Physical violence
    (*b*) Harassment
    (*c*) Loss of employment
    (*d*) Legal problems
    (*e*) Any other.....................................

III. Newspaper Coverage of Environmental Issues

47. Do you think society learns much about environment through newspapers?
    (a) Yes
    (b) No
    (c) Can't say

48. If yes, do you think environmental reports have any influence on the society?
    (a) Yes
    (b) No
    (c) Can't say

49. If so, who will be influenced most?
    (a) Government politicians
    (b) Readers
    (c) NGOs
    (d) Any other....................................

50. What kinds of news stories do you think readers in Kerala seek from newspapers? (Please rank your response)

S.No. Kind of Stories	*Rank*
(a) Political	
(b) Human interest	
(c) Environment	
(d) Sensational/Crime	
(e) Entertainment	
(f) Any other....................................	

51. How do you describe the quality of environmental reporting in Kerala newspapers?
    (a) Very good
    (b) Good
    (c) Poor
    (d) Very poor

52. How do you describe the coverage given to the following major environmental issues by Kerala newspapers?

S.No.	*Major Issues*	*High*	*Medium*	*Low*
(*a*)	Industrial pollution			
(*b*)	Drying up of rivers			
(*c*)	Hazardous solid waste disposal			
(*d*)	Use of pesticides			
(*e*)	Chemical waste			
(*f*)	Destruction of paddy fields			
(*g*)	Pollution of rivers/backwaters			
(*h*)	Destruction of hills			
(*i*)	Deforestation			
(*j*)	Sand mining			
(*k*)	Any other....................................			

53. In reporting on environmental reports, how do you prefer to write? (For example: as a feature, news item, interview etc.)

54. Do you think better training in environmental issues is required for journalists?
    (*a*) Yes
    (*b*) No
    (*c*) Can't say

55. If yes, what type of training do you think is useful to journalists to improve writing?
    (*a*) Periodic training
    (*b*) Special courses on environment
    (*c*) Exposure to expert's lectures
    (*d*) Any other....................................

56. Do you think newspaper management can play a key role in promoting coverage of environment?
    (*a*) Yes
    (*b*) No
    (*c*) Can't say

57. If yes, how can newspaper management support coverage of environmental issues?

    ....

IV. Perception of Journalists

58. In what way can newspapers in Kerala support environment?
    (*a*) By creating awareness among readers on environment through wider coverage
    (*b*) By undertaking special themes or slogans on environment on a regular basis
    (*c*) By giving prominence to environmental stories in the paper
    (*d*) By making investigative studies on issues
    (*e*) Any other....................................

59. What do you think are the important environmental issues in Kerala? (Please rank your response)

S.No.	*Issues*	*Rank*
(*a*)	Industrial pollution	
(*b*)	Drying up of rivers	
(*c*)	Hazardous solid waste disposal	
(*d*)	Use of pesticides	
(*e*)	Chemical waste	
(*f*)	Destruction of paddy fields	
(*g*)	Pollution of rivers/backwaters	
(*h*)	Destruction of hills	
(*i*)	Deforestation	
(*j*)	Sand mining	
(*k*)	Any other..................................	

60. Please cite one specific environmental issue, you think, newspapers in Kerala have projected well in the last five years i.e. during 2001-06

61. Do you think journalists can influence the management to take up reporting on environmental campaigns?
    (*a*) Yes
    (*b*) No
    (*c*) Can't say

62. Do you think journalist's commitment to environment will improve reporting?

(*a*) Yes
(*b*) No
(*c*) Can't say

63. If yes, how can they improve?

64. What do you think is the most important source to cover the following environmental issues? (Please tick your response)

Issues	*Sources*					
	Government	*Business*	*Citizens*	*NGOs*	*Research Agencies*	*Any Other*
(*a*) Industrial pollution						
(*b*) Drying up of rivers						
(*c*) Hazardous solid waste disposal						
(*d*) Use of pesticides						
(*e*) Chemical waste						
(*f*) Destruction of paddy fields						
(*g*) Pollution of rivers/ backwaters						
(*h*) Destruction of hills						
(*i*) Deforestation						
(*j*) Sand mining						
(*k*) Any other......................................						

65. Do you think newspapers in Kerala have increased awareness on environmental issues among the people?
(*a*) Yes
(*b*) No
(*c*) Can't say

66. Do you think literacy programmes in Kerala have helped awareness on environment?
(*a*) Yes
(*b*) No
(*c*) Can't say

67. In what way do you think newspapers can project environment as an important issue?
    (*a*) Having special issues/regular columns on environment
    (*b*) Carrying environment reports on front page with prominent headlines
    (*c*) By setting up special environment team of journalists to cover issues
    (*d*) Undertaking special campaigns to initiate public dialogue
    (*e*) Any other....................................

68. Which mass media do you think is effective in creating awareness on environment? (Please rank your response)

S.No.	*Mass Media*	*Rank*
(*a*)	Newspapers	
(*b*)	TV	
(*c*)	Radio	
(*d*)	Books	
(*e*)	Internet	
(*f*)	Traditional media	
(*g*)	Any other....................................	

69. Do you think photographs can increase readership of environmental issues?
    (*a*) Yes
    (*b*) No
    (*c*) Can't say

70. Do you think special incentives from the Government will encourage environmental reporting?
    (*a*) Yes
    (*b*) No
    (*c*) Can't say

71. If yes, what do you think the best incentive can be? (Please tick any **one** response)
    (*a*) Special cash awards
    (*b*) Free transport facilities

(*c*) Free training on environment
(*d*) Any other..

72. Do you think that newspapers can focus simultaneously on many issues at a time?
(*a*) Yes
(*b*) No
(*c*) Can't say

73. What kind of treatment can environmental stories be given to improve readership? (Please rank your response)

S.No. *Treatment* *Rank*

(*a*) By publishing them on the front page
(*b*) By giving attractive headlines
(*c*) As box items
(*d*) By publishing special pull-outs
(*e*) Any other....................................

74. Do you think newspapers can support initiatives on environmental education? (for example in schools and at grassroots level)
(*a*) Yes
(*b*) No
(*c*) Can't say

75. If yes, how can they support such initiatives?
(*a*) By giving better coverage on such initiatives
(*b*) By encouraging schools to undertake nature campaigns
(*c*) Through partnerships with other mass media to create awareness on environment
(*d*) Supporting folk media in spreading awareness
(*e*) Any other....................................

Please give your suggestions to improve environmental reporting in Kerala

Date:

Time: **Place:**

Bibliography

Ader, C.R. (1995). A Longitudinal Study of Agenda Setting for the Issue of Environmental Pollution, *Journalism and Mass Communication Quarterly, 72:* 300-11.

Afghan, D. and Munuve, J. (2006, June). Report on the Situation Analysis Survey on Media Coverage of Environmental Issues in East Africa (Lake Victoria Basin). Occasional paper.

Agarwal, A., Narain, S., Sharma, A. and Imchen, A. (eds.) (2000). *Poles Apart: Global Environmental Negotiations,* New Delhi: Centre for Science and Environment.

American Opinion Research Inc., (1993). *The Press and the Environment: How Journalists Evaluate Environmental Reporting,* Princeton, NJ: Foundation for American Communications.

Anam, M. (2002). The Media and Development in Bangladesh in *The Right to Tell: The Role of Mass Media in Economic Development,* (pp. 267-274), The World Bank, Washington: The International Bank for Reconstruction and Development.

Anderson, A. (1991). Source Strategies and the Communication of Environmental Affairs, *Media, Culture and Society,* 13(4): 459-76.

Anderson, A. (1997). *Media, Culture and the Environment,* New Jersey: Rutgers University Press.

Anonymous (2008a). A Poisoned River Means a Dying Population, accessed on March 9, 2008 on www.irenees.net.

Anonymous (2008b). Pepsi Plant Indicted for Polluting Groundwater in Kerala, *Down to Earth,* Science and Environment Online, accessed on March 9, 2008 on www.cse.org

Anonymous (2008c). Industrial, Domestic Wastes Polluting Kerala Rivers: Study, *The Hindu Business Line,* accessed on March 9, 2008 on www.thebusinessline.com

Askari, E. (1995). Readers Thirst for more about their Environment, *American Editor, 771*: 14-16.

Atwater, T., Salwen, M.B. and Anderson, R.B. (1985). Media Agenda-setting with Environmental Issues, *Journalism Quarterly, 62*: 393-397.

Bandyopadhyay and Shiva, V. (1989). Development, Poverty and the Growth of the Green Movements in India, *The Ecologist, 19* (3), 111-17.

Banwari (1991). *Pancavati: Indian Approach to Environment,* New Delhi: Shri Vinayaka Publications.

Batterbury, S. (2003, November) Environmental Activism and Social Networks: Campaigning for Bicycles and Alternative Transport in West London, *The Annals of the American Academy of Political and Social Science, 590*: 150-169.

Bell, A. (1994). Media (mis)communication on the Science of Climate Change, *Public Understanding of Science,* 3 (3), 259-275.

Bendix, J., and Liebler, C.M. (1991). Environmental Degradation in Brazilian Amazonia: Perspectives in U.S. News Media, *The Professional Geographer, 43*: 474-85.

Berkowitz, D. and Beach, D.W. (1993). News Sources and News Context: The Effect of Routine News, Conflict and Proximity, *Journalism Quarterly, 70*: 4-12.

Bowman, C. (1996). Needed: A Recommitment. *Nieman Reports, 50*: 5-8.

Brosius, H.B. and Kepplinger H.M. (1990). The Agenda-setting Function of Television News. *Communication Research, 17*(2), 183-211.

Brown, J.D., Bybee, C.R., Weardon, S.T. and Straughan, D.M. (1987). Invisible Power: Newspaper News Sources and the Limits of Diversity, *Journalism Quarterly*, *64*: 45-54.

Brown, L. (2003). *Plan B: Rescuing a Planet under Stress and a Civilization in Trouble*, New York: W. W. Norton and Company.

Brundtland, G.H. (1989). 'Global Change and Our Common Future' in C.S. Silver and R.S. DeFries (eds.), *'One Earth, One Future: Our Changing Global Environment* (pp. 140-147), New Delhi: Affiliated East-West Press Ltd.

Budd, R., Thorp, K.R. and Donohew, L. (1967). *Content Analysis of Communications*, New York: Macmillan.

Byrd, T. (1997). Variation in Environmental Risk Perceptions and Information Sources Among Three Communities in El Paso, *8 Risk: Health, Safety & Environment*, 355.

Cambridge, V.C. (2002). Milestones in Communication and National Development in Y. R. Kamalipour (ed.), (pp. 141-160), *Global Communication*, London: Wadsworth.

Carmody, K. (1995). It's a Jungle Out There. *Columbia Journalism Review*, *34*: 40-45.

Casey, B., Casey, N., Calert, B., French, L. and Lewis, J. (2002). *Television Studies: The Key Concepts*, London: Routledge.

Castells, M. (1983). The City and the Grassroots. A Cross-cultural Theory of Urban Social Movements, Berkeley: University of California Press.

Chan, K. (1999). Hong Kong 1983-95, *International Journal of Public Opinion Research*, *11* (2): 135-151(17).

Chattopadhyay, S. and Franke, R.W. (2006). *Striving for Sustainability, Environmental Stress and Democratic Initiatives in Kerala*, New Delhi: Concept Publishing Company.

Clemencon, R. (2008). The Bali Road Map A First Step on the Difficult Journey to a Post-Kyoto Protocol Agreement, *The Journal of Environment and Development*, 17 (1): 70-94.

Cohen, B.C. (1963). *The Press and Foreign Policy*, Princeton, NJ: Princeton University Press.

Collins, M.F. and T.M. Pharoah. (1974). *Transport Organisation in a Great City: The Case of London*, London: Allen and Unwin.

Commoner, B. (1963). *The Closing Circle*, London: Cape.

Coulson, D.C. and Lacy, S. (1996). Journalists' Perceptions of How Newspaper and Broadcast News Competition Affects Newspaper Content, *Journalism and Mass Communication Quarterly 73* (2): 354-363.

Cox, R. (2006). *Environmental Communication and the Public Sphere*, Thousand Oaks, CA: Sage Publications.

Crawley, C.E. (2007). Localized Debates of Agricultural Biotechnology in Community Newspapers: A Quantitative Content Analysis of Media Frames and Sources, *Science Communication, 28* (3): 314-346.

Davis, J.J. (1995). The Effects of Message Framing on Response to Environmental Communications, *Journalism and Mass Communication Quarterly, 72*: 285-99.

DeFleur, M.L. and Ball-Rokeach, S. (1989). Theories of Mass Communication (fifth edition), New York: Longman Inc.

Detjen J., Fico F., Li X. and Kim Y. (2000). Changing Work Environment of Environmental Reporters, *Newspaper Research Journal, 21* (1), 2-12.

Detjen, J. (2001, Third Quarter). Environment Back on Front Page, *IPI Global Journalist*, pp. 16-17.

Dudo, A.D., Dahlstrom, M.F. and Brossard, D. (2007). Reporting a Potential Pandemic, A Risk-Related Assessment of Avian Influenza Coverage in U.S. Newspapers, *Science Communication, 28* (4): 429-454.

Dunwoody, S. and Griffin, R.J. (1993). Journalistic Strategies for Reporting Long-Term Environmental Issues: A Case Study of Three Superfund Sites in A. Hansen (ed.), (pp. 22-50), *The Mass Media and Environmental Issues*, Leicester, England: Leicester University Press.

Dunwoody, S. and Peters, H. (1992). Mass Media Coverage of Technological and Environmental Risks: A Survey of Research in the United States and Germany. *Public Understanding of Science 1* (3), 199-230.

Ehrlich, P. and Ehrlich A. (1970). *Population, Resources, Environment,* San Francisco: W. H. Freeman.

Entman, R.M. (1993). Framing: Toward Clarification of a Fractured Paradigm, *Journal of Communication, 43*: 51-58.

Expert Corner Report, (undated). A New Model of Environmental Communication for Europe from Consumption to Use of Information, Prepared for the European Environment Agency.

Franke, R.W. and Chasin, B.H. (1992). *Kerala: Development Through Radical Reform,* New Delhi: Promilla and Co.

Friedman, S.M. (1986). The Journalist's World in S.M. Friedman and S. Dunwoody (eds.) *Scientists and Journalists,* New York: Free Press (pp. 17-41).

Friedman, S.M., Gorney, C.M., and Egolf, B.P. (1987). Reporting on Radiation: A Content Analysis of Chernobyl Coverage, *Journal of Communication, 37,* 58-79.

Friedman, S.M. (1991). Two Decades of the Environmental Beat. In C.L. LaMay and E.E. Dennis(ed.) *Media and the Environment,* (pp. 17-28), Washington: Island Press.

Friedman, S.M., Gorney, C.M. and Egolf, B.P. (1992). Chernobyl Coverage: How the U.S. Media Treated the Nuclear Industry, *Public Understanding of Science,* 1 (3): 305-323.

Fura, Z. (1985). "Institutions: The Polish Ecological Club", *Environment, 27* (9), 4-5, 43.

Futehally, Z. (1977). *Report of the Task Force for the Ecological Planning for the Western Ghats,* NCEPC.

Gale, R.P. (1987). Calculating Risk: Radiation and Chernobyl, *Journal of Communication, 37,* 68-73.

Gooch, G.D. (1996). Environmental Concern and the Swedish Press, A Case Study of the Effects of Newspaper Reporting, Personal

Experience and Social Interaction on the Public's Perception of Environmental Risks, *European Journal of Communication, 11* (1), 107-127.

Gopikrishna, S. and Sasi Kumar, K. (2006). Solid Waste: Management Issues and Suggestions for Kerala Conditions, *Kerala Calling, 26* (11), 12-15.

Graham, J.D. and Dziuban, P.R. (1996). Why Important Stories are Underreported. *Neiman Reports,* 50: 27-28.

Graham, K. and Chandler, G. (2000). *Environmental Heroes: Success Stories of People at Work for the Earth,* New Delhi, Mcmillan.

Guedes, O. (2000). Environmental Issues in the Brazilian Press, *Gazette, 62*(6): 537-554.

Guha, R. (1991). *The Unquiet Woods: A History of Social Movements in Uttarakhand,* Delhi: Oxford University Press.

Guha, R. (2002, March). A Brief History of Environmental Journalism, *Humanscape,* 37-38.

Hackett, R. and Zhao, Y. (1998). *Sustaining Democracy: Journalism and the Politics of Objectivity,* Toronto: Garamond Press.

Hali, R. (2006). Elimination of Rice Fields, *Kerala Calling, 26* (11), 28-29.

Hansen, A. (1991). The Media and the Social Construction of Environment, *Media, Culture and Society,* 13, 443-458.

Hansen, A. (1994). Journalistic Practices and Science Reporting in the British Press, *Public Understanding of Science, 3* (2), 111-134.

Harvey, B. and Hallet, J.D. (1977). *The Environmental Debate: Environment and Society, An Introductory Analysis,* London and Basingstoke: The Macmillan Press Ltd.

Haque, M. (1986). 'Is Development News more Salient than Human Interest Stories in Indian elite press?' *Gazette, 38* (3): 83-99.

Held, D. (2005). Globalization: The Dangers and Answers. In David Held *et al.,* (ed.) *Debating Globalization,* Cambridge: Polity Press.

Hensman, R. (2004). Globalization, Women and Work: What are we talking about?, *Economic and Political Weekly,* XXXIX (10): 1030-1034.

Hester, J.B. and Gonzenbach, W.J. (1995). The Environment: TV News, Real-World Cues, and Public Opinion Over Time, *Mass Comm. Review*, 22: 5-20.

Indiradevi, P.I. (2007, February). Pesticide Use in the Rice Bowl of Kerala: Health Costs and Policy Options, South Asian Network for Development and Environmental Economics, Working Paper No. 20-07.

Iyengar, S. and Kinder, D.R. (1987). *News that Matters: Television and American Opinion*, Chicago: University of Chicago Press.

Iyengar, S. and Simon, A. (1997). News Coverage of the Gulf Crisis and Public Opinion: A study of Agenda-setting, Priming and Framing. In Shanto Iyengar and Richard Reeves (eds.) *Do the Media Govern? Politicians, Voters and Reporters in America* (pp. 248-257), London: Sage.

Kabala, S. (1985). "Poland: Facing the Hidden Costs of Development". *Environment*, 27 (9), 6-13, 37-42.

Khanna and Nath, G. (1990). *Global Environmental Crisis and Management*, New Delhi: Ashish.

Kitzinger, J. and Reilly, J. (1997). The Rise and Fall of Risk Reporting, Media Coverage of Human Genetics Research, 'False Memory Syndrome' and 'Mad Cow Disease', *European Journal of Communication*, 12 (3), 319-350.

Lacy, S. and Coulson, D. (2000). Comparative Case Study, Newspaper Source Use on the Environmental Beat, *Newspaper Research Journal*, 21 (1), 13-25.

Lerner, D. (1958). *The Passing of Traditional Society*, New York: Free Press.

Liebler, C.M. and Bendix, J. (1996). Old-Growth Forests on Network News: News Sources and Framing of an Environmental Controversy. *Journalism and Mass Communication Quarterly*, 73 (1): 53-65.

Litman, T. (1999). *Reinventing Transportation: Exploring the Paradigm Shift Needed to Reconcile Transportation and Sustainability Objectives*. www.vtpi.org/reinvent.pdg

Logan, R.A. (2001, Third Quarter). How Reporters Miss the Point, *IPI Global Journalist*, pp. 24.

Logan, R.A., Shin J. and Park, J. (2004). Prevailing Impressions of Social Actors in Korean News Coverage of a Public Health Crisis, *Science Communication*, *25* (4), 399-416.

Love, A. (1990, Winter). The Production of Environmental Meanings in the Media: A New Era. *Media Education Journal*, *10*, 18-20.

Major, A.M. and Atwood, L.E. (2004). Environmental Risks in the News: Issues, Sources, Problems, and Values, *Public Understanding of Science*, *13* (3), 295-308.

Mazoomdar, J. (2006). Media and Environmental Issues in AshaRani Mathur (ed.) *Indian Media, Illusion, Delusion and Reality, Essays in Honour of Prem Bhatia*, (pp. 158-165), New Delhi: Rupa and Co.

Mazur, A. and Lee, J. (1993). Sounding the Global Alarm: Environmental Issues in the U.S. National News, *Social Studies of Science*, *23*: 681-720.

Melkote, S.R. and Steeves, H.L. (2001). *Communication for Development in the Third World: Theory and Practice for Empowerment*, New Delhi: Sage Publications.

Merten, K., Peters, H.P. and Klosse, K. (1990). *Risk Information on the Chernobyl Disaster in the West German Media*. Paper presented at the XIIth World Congress of Sociology, Madrid, 9-13 July.

Mikami, S., Takeshita, T., Nakada, M. and Kawabata, M. (1995). The Media Coverage and Public Awareness of Environmental Issues in Japan, *International Communication Gazette*, *54* (3), 209-226.

Mitra, A. (2001). Popular Movements: Chipko, *Down to Earth*, (special issue) New Delhi: Centre for Science and Environment, pp. 26-29.

Molotch, H. and Lester, M. (1974). News as Purposive Behavior: On the Strategic Use of Routine Events, Accidents and Scandals. *American Sociological Review*, *39*: 101-12.

Murthy, D.V.R. (2000). Development News in Indian Newspapers: An Analysis of Select Dailies, *Media Asia*, *27* (1): 24-29, 53.

Murthy, D.V.R. (2005). *Media and Accountability: An Overview,* New Delhi: Kanishka Publishers.

Murthy, D.V.R. (2006). *Development Journalism: What Next?,* New Delhi: Kanishka Publishers.

Nair, G.K. (2005, September). Deforestation, Sand Mining Bring Water Table Down, cited in www.thehindubusinessline.com.

Norhstedt, S.A. (1991). The Information Crisis in Sweden after Chernobyl, *Media, Culture and Society, 13* (4), 477-97.

North, R.C., Holsti, O., Zaninivich, M.G. and Zinnes, D.A. (1963). *Content Analysis: A Handbook with Applications for the Study of International Crisis,* Evanston: North Western University Press.

Ohkura, Y. (1995). The Roles and Limitations of Newspapers in Environmental Reporting: Case study: Isahaya Bay Land Reclamation Project Issue: *Marine Pollution Bulletin, 47,* issues 1-6, January-June 2003, (pp. 237-245), Environmental Management of Enclosed Coastal Seas.

Pan, Z. and Kosicki, G.M. (1993). Framing Analysis: An Approach to News Discourse, *Political Communication, 10*: 55-75.

Park, J. (2001, Third Quarter). Journalist's Journal: The Up and Down of Korean Environmental Journalism, *IPI Global Journalist,* p. 3.

Parlour, J.W. and Schatow, S. (1978). The Mass Media and Public Concern for Environmental Problems in Canada 1960-1972. *International Journal of Environmental Studies, 13,* 9-17.

Perdue, W. (1995). *Paradox of Change* (Westport, CT: Praeger).

Preetha, L. and Karipai, R.S. (1996). Analysis of Farm News Coverage in Dailies, *Communicator, XXXI* (1): 25-27.

Prime, R. (1992). *The World Forest Section A, Learning from the Tradition, Hinduism and Ecology Seeds of Truth,* England: Cassel Publishers Limited.

Pritchard, D. (1991). The Role of Press Councils in a System of Media Accountability: The Case of Quebec, *Canadian Journal of Communication,* 16.

Pritchard, D. (2000). The Process of Media Accountability. In D. Pritchard (ed.) *Holding the Media Accountable: Citizens, Ethics and the Law* (pp. 1-10). Indianapolis: Indiana University Press.

Protess, D.L., Cook, F.L., Curtin, T.R., Gordon, M.T., Leff, D.R., McCombs, M.E. and Miller, P. (1987). The impact of investigating reporting on public opinion and policy making: targeting toxic waste. *Public Opinion Quarterly, 51,* 166-85.

Rajalakshmi, N. and Birundha, D. (1994). *Environomics: Economic Analysis of Environment,* New Delhi: Allied Publishers.

Ramachandran, V.K. (1996). 'On Kerala's Development Achievements,' in Jean Dreze and Amartya Sen (eds.), *Indian Development: Selected Regional Perspectives,* Oxford: Clarendon Press.

Reis, R. (1999). Environmental News Coverage of the Earth Summit by Brazilian Newspapers, *Science Communication, 21* (2), 137-155.

Remnick, D. (1991). "Stalin's Lethal Legacy of Filth." *The Washington Post* (May 21), P. A1.

Riffe, D., Sust, C.F. and Lacy, S.R. (1993). The Effectiveness of Random, Consecutive Week and Constructive Sampling in Newspaper Content Analysis. *Journalism Quarterly, 70* (1): 133-139.

Roche, J.P. and Muskavitch, M.A.T. (2003). Limited Precision in Print Media Communication of West Nile Virus Risks, *Science Communication, 24* (3), 353-365.

Rogers, P. (2002, Winter). Complexity in Environment Reporting is Critical to Public Decision-Making, *Nieman Reports,* 32-34.

Ross, S.D. (1998). "Their Rising Voices": A Study of Civil Rights, Social Movements, and Adverting in the New York Times. *Journalism & Mass Communication Quarterly, 75* (3): 518-534.

Rothman, S. and Lichter, R.S. (1990). Elite Ideology and Risk Perception in Nuclear Energy Policy. In Doris A. Graber (ed.) *Media Power in Politics* (second edition) (pp. 346-353), New Delhi: Macmillan.

Rubin, D.M. (1987). How the News Media Reported on Three Mile Island and Chernobyl, *Journal of Communication, 37*, 42-57.

Rubin, D.M. and Sachs, D.P. (1973) *Mass Media and the Environment: Water Resources, Land Use and Atomic Energy in California*. New York: Praegar.

Saari, M.A., Gibson, C. and Osler, C. (1998). Endangered Species: Science Writers in the Canadian Daily Press, *Public Understanding of Science, 7 (1), 61-81.*

Sachsman, D.B. (1976). Public Relations Influence on Coverage of Environment in the San Francisco Area. *Journalism Quarterly, 53*, 54-60.

Sachsman, D.B., Simon, J. and Valenti, J.M. (2002). The Environment Reporters of New England, *Science Communication, 23* (6): 410-441.

Sachsman, D.B., Simon, J. and Valenti, J.M. (2004). Risk and the Environment Reporters: A Four-region Analysis, *Public Understanding of Science*, 13 (4), 399-416.

Sachsman, D.B., Simon, J. and Valenti, J.M. (2006). Regional Issues, National Norms, A Four-Region Analysis of U.S. Environment Reporters, *Science Communication, 28*, (1), 93-121.

Salwen, M.B. (1988). Effect of Accumulation of Coverage on Issue Salience in Agenda-setting, *Journalism Quarterly, 65*, 100-6.

Sandman, P.M., Sachsman, D.B., Greenberg, M.R., Gochfeld, M. and Dunwoody, S. (1987). *Environmental Risk and the Press: An Explanatory Assessment*, New Brunswick, NJ: Transaction Books.

Sawant, S.T. (1993). Managing Environmental Challenge in C.K. Varshney and D. R. Sardesai, (eds.) (pp. 78- 82), *Environmental Challenges*, New Delhi: Wiley Eastern Limited.

Schlesinger, P. (1987). *Putting "Reality" Together: BBC News*. London: Constable.

Schoenfeld, A., Meier R. and Griffin R.J. (October, 1979). Constructing a Social Problem: The Press and the Environment, *Social Problems*, 27 (1), 38-61.

Seitz, J.L. (1990). *The Politics of Development: An Introduction to Global Issues,* Bombay: Popular Prakashan.

Sekhar, T. (1981). Role of Newspapers in Creating Mass Concern with Environmental Issues in India, *International Journal of Environmental Sciences, 17,* 115-20.

"Sendzimir Steel Mill: Albatross of Communication" (1997). *Economic Review* (April 29).

Shaw, D.L. and McCombs, M.E. (1989). 'Dealing with Illicit Drugs: The power and limits of agenda setting', in Pamela Shoemaker (ed.), *Communication Campaigns about Drugs: Government, Media and Public* (pp. 189-201), New Jersey: Lawrence Erlbaum Associates.

Shiva, V. (2002). Water Wars: Privatization, Pollution, and Profit, New Delhi: India Research Press.

Shourie, A. (1995). 'Facts are Sacred, Did You Say?' *Deccan Chronicle,* June 25.

Sigal, L.V. (1986). Sources are the News. In R. Manoff and M. Schudson, (eds.), *Reading the News,* (pp. 9-37), New York: Pantheon.

Sinilal, B. (2007, July). Foundation Strong: But Hurting Nature, *Kerala Calling,* 37-38.

Sleeper, D. (1979). Do the Media Too Often Miss the Message? *Conservation Foundation Letter,* January: 1-8.

Srivastava, M.P. (1996). Coverage of Environment by Print Media, *Communicator, XXXI* (1): 20-24.

Stoez, D., Guzzetta, C., and Lusk, M. (1999). *International Development,* London: Allyn and Bacon.

Strodhoff, G.G., Hawkins, R.P., and Schoenfeld A.C. (1985) Media Roles in a Social Movement: A Model of Ideology Diffusion, *Journal of Communication, 35* (2), 134-53.

Stuyck, S.C., (1990). Public Health and the Media: Unequal Partners? in Charles Atkin and Lawrence Wallack (eds.) *Mass Communication and Public Health, Complexities and Conflicts,* (pp. 71-77), Thousand Oaks, CA: Sage Publications.

Suhonen, P. (1993). Environmental Issues, the Finnish Major Press, and Public Opinion, *International Communication Gazette, 51* (2), 91-112.

Suresh Kumar, K. (undated). Mass Media and Environmental Issues, in *Mass Media and Environment,* Occasional paper published by Department of Journalism and Mass Communication, Pune University, pp. 10-11.

Taylor, C.E., Lee, J. and Davie, W.R. (2000). Local Press Coverage of Environmental Conflict, *Journalism and Mass Communication Quarterly, 77* (1), 175-192.

Tichenor, P.J., Donohue, G.A., and Olien, C.N. (1970). Mass Media Flow and Differential Growth in Knowledge, *Public Opinion Quarterly, 34,* 158-70.

Tiwari, H.N. (1998). *Environmental Law,* Allahabad Law Agency: Faridabad.

Trumbo, C. (1996). Constructing Climate Change: Claims and Frames in U.S. News Coverage of an Environmental Issue, *Public Understanding of Science, 5* (3), 269-283.

Varghese, K.G. (2003). Globalization Traumas and New Social Imaginary: *Visvakarma* Community of Kerala. *Economic and Political Weekly,* XXXVIII (45): 4794-4802.

Venugopal, P.N. (2006, March). Kerala: Rain-blessed and Short of Water, cited in www.indiatogether.org

Vilanilam, J.V. (1993). *Science Communication and Development,* New Delhi: Sage Publications.

Vraneski, A. and Richter, R. (2002). *Frames, Framing, and Reframing In, and Through, the Mass Media: Reflection of Four Protracted Environmental Disputes in the Israeli Press,* Technion IIT. Haifa. Israel, ICAR Working Paper #21.

Wakefield, S.E.L. and Elliott, S.J. (2003). Constructing the News: The Role of Local Newspapers in Environmental Risk Communication, *The Professional Geographer, 55* (2), 216-226.

West, B., Lewis, J. and Greenberg, M. (2001). Journalist's Views of the Environment: Issues and Challenges, *12 Risk: Health, Safety and Environment*, 299-310.

Wilkins, L. and Patterson, P. (1987). Risk Analysis and the Construction of News, *Journal of Communication*, 37, 80-92.

Wilson, K.M. (2000). Drought, Debate, and Uncertainty: Measuring Reporters' Knowledge and Ignorance about Climate Change, *Public Understanding of Science*, 9 (1), 1-13.

Witt, W. (1974, Winter). The Environmental Reporter on U.S. Daily Newspapers, *Journalism Quarterly*, 697-704.

www.cleankerala.org/html/mission.html
www.jalanidhi.com/health.htm
www.indiatogether.org
www.unep.org

Index

Afforestation, 165, 167
Agenda-setting hypothesis, 31
Agenda-setting role, 14, 32
Anti-nuclear statements, 28
Arsenic contamination, 17
Awareness campaigns, 50

Backwaters, 78, 79, 87, 93, 99, 174-75
Beat reporter, 132
Biological life, 8
Bombay Natural History Society, 170
Breathing problems, 173
Brundtland report, 4
Bushy hilly terrains, 174, 176

Camden Cycle Campaign, 11
Catchment areas, 176
Centre of Environmental Communication Studies, 33
Chaliyar river, 103
Chemical fertilizers, Indiscriminate use, 173
Chernobyl accident, 28
China clay mining, 120
Chipko movement, 2, 166-68
Climate change, 5, 26, 27, 50
Coastal environment, 175
Code sheet, 51
Community
  misunderstanding, 23
  newspapers, 27
Competing dailies, 33
Construction activities, 174-76
Content analysis, 15, 23, 38, 47, 51, 83, 111, 144, 146, 156, 160-61
Copy tester, 44
Corporate pressure, 122
Court proceedings, 50, 158, 160
Coverage of environmental issues, 84

Dams, 6, 12, 18, 24, 168-69
Deforestation, 4, 5, 14, 79, 93, 94, 99, 120, 167-68, 172, 175-76
Deshabhimani, 37, 42, 44, 52, 53, 55, 59-61, 67, 68, 70, 71, 74, 76, 87, 97, 99, 113-14, 156
Destruction of hills, 78, 79, 93
Drinking water pollution, 51, 114-16, 157
Drinking water problem, 94, 132, 134

Ealing Cycling Campaign, 11
Earth Summit, 4, 5, 31, 143

Ecological
awareness, 50
movement, 166, 168
Economic growth, 3, 4
Encroached land, 134
Endosulphan pesticide, 94, 97, 99, 101, 103
English newspapers, 41, 42, 46, 133
Environmental
activists, 23, 24
agencies, 76, 151
awareness, 84, 107, 109, 122, 127, 157, 163, 165
beat, 21, 25, 26, 69, 71, 72, 83, 91, 137, 148-49, 158
campaigns, 32, 103, 111
catastrophe, 3
conflicts, 32, 66, 67, 91, 131, 139, 148
consequences, 6
controversies, 67
coverage, 21, 32, 69, 86, 148, 153, 157
degradation, 50
destruction, 1, 161
deterioration, 4, 32
disasters, 17, 23, 175
education, 4, 50, 110, 114, 116, 128, 156, 164-65
group, 9, 23
information, 33, 34, 36, 75, 143, 157
initiatives, 4
issue surfaces, 66, 67, 161
items, 23
journalism, 18
journalism, 18
Journalist, 22, 33, 69, 90, 139, 148, 154
living, 72
management, 130
movements, 2, 11, 165
news, 23, 27-30, 50, 66, 67, 85, 90, 122, 140, 146-48, 154, 158, 161-62
NGOs, 65
perspectives, 27
pollution, 31
pressure group, 35
problems, 4, 10, 22, 31, 33, 40, 67, 68, 95, 99, 103, 130, 143, 148, 158
reporters, 21, 22, 25, 122-24, 128, 132, 158, 161
reporting, 65
reports, 66, 85, 125, 148, 153, 160
risks, 25, 28, 30, 31
science, 75
security, 11
stories, 21-23, 25, 26, 92, 108, 119, 122, 124, 154, 158
tax, 31
team, 32
threat, 132
transmitters, 34
values, 30
Environmentalism, 2
Environmentalists, 10, 25, 169
Ernakulam district, 99
European environmental communicators, 33
Evergreen forests, 126, 139
E-waste, 132
Expert Corner Report, 33

Farm news, 27
Federal state, 12
Female journalists, 55, 146
Fertilizers, 135, 171, 173-74
Forests, 1-3, 41, 50, 103, 127, 134, 138, 142, 167-69, 175-76
auction, 167
department, 127
encroachment, 94, 99
fires, 51
resources, 51, 166
tract, 168
Forestland, 94, 126, 175

German media, 29
Globalization, 11, 12, 14
Gopeshwar, 167
Greenpeace, 171, 173
Groundwater, 171, 173, 175-76

Hazardous waste disposal, 51, 113, 115, 156
Health crisis, 26
Hindustan Coca Cola Beverages Ltd, 24
Hindustan Insecticides Limited, 122
Hindustan Times, 124
Holsti formula, 51
Human induced problems, 172
Human interest stories, 50, 160-61
Human wastes, 174-75

Indian Express, 7, 123-24, 133
Industrial pollution, 1, 50, 78, 79, 87, 93, 140, 171
Inter-coder reliability, 51
Inter-governmental conference, 4
International environment group, 171
Investigative journalism, 23

Journalistic
  career, 125, 130
  judgment, 34
  neglect, 26
Journalists
  broadcast, 21
  exclusive, 159
  fellow, 124
  objective, 22
  quality press, 34
  specialized, 34

Kairali TV, 41, 43
Karamana River, 97
Kasargode district, 94
Kerala Kaumudi, 37, 41, 42, 44, 52, 53, 55, 59, 61, 67, 68, 70, 71, 74, 76, 87, 97, 99, 115-17
Kerala newspapers report, 67
Kerala Sanchari and Bharath Vilasam, 43
Kerala Sastra Sahitya Parishad, 13, 133, 169
Kerala State Council for Science Technology, 174
Kerala State Health Department, 24
Kerala Tourism Development Corporation, 127
Killi River, 97
Kottayam, 42, 44, 48, 49, 53, 95, 99, 111, 113-14, 143, 146, 156-57
Kozhikode, 41, 43, 44, 48, 49, 53, 95, 103, 111, 113-14, 116, 129, 143, 146, 156-57

Lackadaisical attitude, 158
Literacy and Environmental Awareness, 109
Litter-free cities, 103
Local environmental problems, 31
London, 10, 11

Malayalam newspapers, 41, 43, 46
Mandal forest, 166
Mangrove forests, 120
Mathrubhumi, 37, 41, 42, 44, 52-55, 58, 59, 61, 68, 70, 71, 74-76, 97, 99, 101, 103, 115-17, 135
Media
  coverage, 18, 32, 35
  organization, 65
  stories, 18
Meenachil river, 99
Modernization, 9-11
Multinational company, 137, 165
Multiple sources, 159
Multi-sourcing, 134

Natural environment, 3, 5
Natural forests, 2

New Indian Express, 23, 37, 41-44, 48, 49, 52, 53, 55, 58-61, 67, 68, 71, 74, 87, 97, 101, 103, 115
News editor, 124, 128, 130
Newspaper
  campaigns, 129
  competition, 33
  coverage, 20, 27, 34, 107, 136, 155
  daily English-language, 22
  financial, 124
  highlight, 137
  influence, 84
  management, 65, 90, 139, 153-54, 163
  readers, 65, 84, 125, 152, 159
  regional, 133
  religious, 133
  reports, 17, 137, 139
NGOs, 18, 78, 79, 85, 110, 133-34, 151, 153, 158-59
Nila river, 172
Non-environment stories, 25
Non-existing sources, 81, 152
Non-governmental organizations, 110, 165
North American newspapers, 30
Nowa Huta, 7-9
Nuclear industries, 28
Nuclear power, 28

Online newspaper journalists, 15

Paddy fields, 87, 135, 174-76
  destruction of, 51, 78, 94
  reported destruction of, 93, 97, 101
Perceptions of
  accountability, 38, 144
  environmental reporting, 38, 74, 144, 150
  journalists, 33, 37, 46, 143, 145, 158
Perennial rivers, 172
Periyar river, 101, 134, 171, 174
Pesticides, 41, 51, 78, 87, 93, 130, 163, 171, 173-74
Phata-Rampur forest, 167
Plachimada Coca Cola issue, 94, 97, 99
Policy-makers, 14, 157
Population growth, 3, 14, 172
Predominant sources, 157
Professional obligations, 38, 46, 64, 144-45, 147
Proof reader, 44
Public awareness, 17, 31, 169
Public campaign, 13
Public perceptions, 157
Public transport, 10

Quality of environmental reporting, 86, 153
Quality of life, 3, 4, 143

Random sampling method, 161
Renewable natural resource, 168
Research design, 144
Research methodology, 37
Rice culture, 174
Risk
  communication, 28-30
  information, 28, 30
  magnitude, 29
River basins, 176
River pollution, 50, 51, 78, 79, 87, 95, 114-15, 157, 163, 174
River sand mining, 41
Riverbeds, 17, 176
Role of Media, 110, 156

Sachsman, 21, 25, 161
Sahyadri Development Society, 127
Sampling Procedure, 48
Sand mining, 51, 78, 93, 94, 96, 97, 101, 104, 116, 137, 160, 162, 172, 176
Save our Seals campaign, 15
Save Silent Valley Campaign, 12

Science journalism, 22
Self-efficacy, 29
Silent Valley, 13, 123, 127, 168-69
Skin problems, 173
Social forestry, 165
Social movements, 12-14, 165
Social problems, 36
Solid waste, 78, 158, 172
Special correspondent, 124-25, 127, 134
Special incentives, 108-9, 155-56, 161
Specialist journalists, 34
Steel mills, 7, 8
Stockholm Conference, 165-66
Subject categories, 50, 51, 114-17, 146
Survey method, 38, 39, 144
Surya TV, 41
Sustainable development, 4, 11
Swedish newspapers, 32

Tehri Garhwal, 167
Telugu newspapers, 28
Thiruvananthapuram Kottayam, 41
Times of India, 18, 42, 123, 125-26
Trainee journalist, 129, 131, 133, 138
Training period, 138
Tropical rainforest, 39
Tyndall report, 66

Underground water table, 176
United Nations Conference of World Leaders on Human Environment, 143
United Nations Conference on Environment and Development, 5, 31
United Nations Environment Programme, 4
United Nations Framework Convention on Climate Change, 5
United News of India, 126
Urbanization, 6, 10, 99
USA, 4, 15, 21, 25, 28, 33

Vanishing forests, 175
Vested interests, 67, 81, 139-40, 148, 152, 168
Vision problems, 135, 173
Vistula river, 8

Waste disposal, 36, 94, 99, 102, 158
Wastewater, 99
Water resources, 6, 101, 143, 172
Water scarcity, 175-76
Water theme park, 122
Well-projected issue, 94, 95, 99
West Nile, 30
Wild life, 138
Women journalists, 132
Working Journalist Act, 43
World Commission on Environment and Development, 4
World Leaders on Human Environment, 4

Youth channel, 41
Youth Times, 125-26